Rob Taylerson

I COME TO DO YOUR WILL

Christian Discernment Through the Heritage and Tradition of the Church

Oscott Series 11

VERITAS

Published 2000 by Veritas Publications
7-8 Lower Abbey Street
Dublin 1

Copyright © Rob Taylerson, 2000

ISBN 1 85390 506 2

British Library Cataloguing
in Publication Data.
A catalogue record for
this book is available
from the British Library.

Cover design by Bill Bolger
Printed in the Republic of Ireland by Betaprint Ltd, Dublin

CONTENTS

Introduction   7

1. The Vision of Hope and the Presence of Jesus   9
2. Relationship with God   15
3. Personal Stages of Faith and Choice   20
4. Prayer, Listening, and Choice   25
5. Norms of Life and Norms of Action   31
6. Choosing with God in the Old Testament
    and in the New   39
7. Prophets, Prophecy and Signs from God   46
8. What is God's Will?   53
9. Charisms   61
10. The Ignatian Method of Discernment   68
11. Recognising Sin   75
12. Being Off-Balance   85
13. The Energy of Passions   93
14. The Dynamics of Conscience   100
15. Friends and Decisions   108
16. Christian Community and Choice   118
17. Truth and Revelation   125
18. In Conclusion   134

I am grateful to many people for their support and help in writing this book. Among many who have given their time and expertise, I would particularly like to thank:

My parents (Peter and Pauline Taylerson), Mrs Anne Shardlow, Fr Peter Conley, Miss Cathy Bennett and Fr David Oakley, for reading, correcting and commenting on the entire manuscript. I am very grateful to Fr Patrick Kilgarriff for editorial comments on behalf of the Oscott-Veritas committee, and to the readers of Veritas, Dublin for their suggestions.

I would also like to thank:

Fr Kenneth Collins, Fr Philip Egan, Fr Gerard Norton OP and Fr Paul Lyons, for their comments and suggestions concerning particular chapters.

INTRODUCTION

In the early Church after the Resurrection, the apostles' ministry took on a vibrant strength, and through them new life came to others. This life came through the presence of the Holy Spirit, guiding and inspiring them. Jesus' followers, for their part, were keen and eager.

By comparison, some of our present-day Christian practice seems limited by uncertainties about what to do and how to live. 'Hesitant' Christianity lacks a wholeness and vitality. The way of life of being 'not quite sure what to do for the best' is not uncommon. A lack of confidence does affect me, and perhaps affects us all. It brings with it several limitations. It doesn't give glory to God or reflect God well in this world. It is often accompanied by a decrease in joy and hope, and an increase in anxiety. I might even see Christian life as a burden to be undertaken, with few right answers, rather than a joy and a liberation to be lived and shared.

How can such hesitancy be avoided? How can we live by the same spirit that inspired the early Church? Unbridled enthusiasm for every idea that comes to mind is a path to ruin. Too much caution, however, which leads to inaction when evil is present, can allow evil to triumph. How do we find the best path? How do we learn what God wants in a way that will not only give us knowledge but will also motivate our hearts and lives into loving and generous action?

This book is a series of reflections. Its themes are wide-ranging. It starts with the basic building-blocks or tools of Christian discernment (courage, hope, focus on Christ, use of scriptures, prayer, the personal spiritual journey, understanding God's will/plan, the meanings of 'discernment' and the ways of Christian choice). Later chapters are more specialised, and look at specific influences such as conscience, friendships, community, problems of personal clarity of vision, the search for truth and revelation. It is hoped that these will be of benefit to the reader in his or her own spiritual life.

Many insights giving answers or direction have come to the Church through the scriptures. Other insights have come through writings of holy men and women down the ages. Such guidance on discernment (including the courage to put discernment into action, and related aspects of spiritual life) is the subject of this book. It is not a book about contemporary ideas, but rather introduces the reader to long-established models and ideas from the tradition and history of the Church to help, to inspire, to evaluate, to understand and to support Christian response to God in daily life.

1

THE VISION OF HOPE AND
THE PRESENCE OF JESUS

My Vision and God's Vision

Three men were doing the same task. Each was hitting a
piece of stone. When asked, 'What are you doing?' each
gave a different answer.

The first said,
'I am sweating.'
The second said,
'I am earning a living'
The third said,
'I am building a cathedral.'[1]

This story is an allegory of Christian action. It shows a range
of understanding of the tasks to be done. Its insight is particularly
helpful when there are dull things to do or demanding choices to
make. It tells of normal Christian life and illustrates authentic
hope.

The allegory can be unwrapped like this:

We don't always understand the implications of the tasks
we carry out. Sometimes we may see only the amount of
effort that a task requires, and cannot see beyond it. If we
do see beyond it, we might only be looking as far as any
immediate reward. The person who understands most
clearly what he or she is doing can see the current task as
part of a divine plan for the future life of the community.

It leads to the following reflections:

> Following Christ often requires continued effort. It involves being called like a labourer to work for God. But most of all it must include the realisation that what God builds is so much greater than the 'little stone I am hitting'. Each of us is a member of the body of Christ, through which God's kingdom is being established. My current actions have a meaning in the kingdom which is not yet complete; that kingdom which my seemingly insignificant tasks can help to build.

This insight gives a great boost to do God's will. People without such a vision can lack the spark to fire them up. Like a car with a flat battery, the courage that should be a driving force just doesn't happen. Without this gift it is easy to be blind to any spiritual meaning; energy will be lacking.

With it, God's light is our energy. Even if some of our tasks may seem dull, hope gives clear vision to our daily activities. With it, we gain impetus and courage. The gift of hope is light, which enables us to see clearly not only what is being built for the future, but also what we're to do now.

The parable also serves as a reminder that the Church and the Kingdom of God, are built up through the community, often by ways of life that might at first seem insignificant. Without this image, despair may reign, or apathy, or rejection of responsibility, or poor self-image, or a lack of respect for others. Vision dims.

Even Christians may, when vision seems limited, only think of God in empty moments or when in a crisis. Hope-vision, which sees God and his kingdom in all circumstances, recognises that all we do relates to God. Hope in God can transform what seems dull or empty into the promise of his future glory. Hope clarifies vision which might otherwise seem cloudy or foolish. Hope can even place the suffering Christ at the heart of any ills. It believes in his resurrection, which overcomes those ills. So hope lifts our hearts when there are difficulties.

Without hope we bear a heavier burden of trials of life than God wants us to carry. Sickness, death, relationship problems, financial worries and hardships can seem so overwhelming and difficult.

Seeing and Walking in Light

God's people are expected to ask for 'light'. When we see by God's light we understand what is happening and gain courage. Phrases from the psalms come to mind, for example:

> . . . in your light we see light (Ps 35:10)

and the opposite:

> . . . having eyes but not seeing (Ps 113:5; 134:16).[2]

These are reminders that first we must want God's vision.

Phrases that talk of 'walking in the light' suggest not only seeing God's will, but carrying out our actions under the energy and strength it gives. The image of God's light represents not only knowledge, or direction, but also courage:

> . . . For you rescued my soul from death, you kept my feet from stumbling that I may walk in the presence of God and enjoy the light of the living (Ps 55:14).

> . . . Happy the people who acclaim such a king, who walk, O Lord, in the light of your face (Ps 88:16).

> . . . O house of Jacob, come, let us walk in the light of the Lord (Isa 2:5).[3]

The image of 'God's light' presented in scripture is a reminder that God always seeks to guide us. Any desire, expressed in prayer, to 'see' God's will, is in itself usually incomplete. Vision without commitment shows a void. With clear vision should come the prayer for the courage to act on the vision, or 'do' it. 'Light' is given not only to see the way, but also to walk in it. Clear vision and personal courage should, in God, be linked.

Unless the follower of Christ is prepared and willing to see the world through God's eyes, faith limps. Zeal, if present, may be misdirected. Unless we long to follow his light with our lives (and that may mean living courageously) we won't be open to doing his will.

The Need for Hope
Christian vision always comes impregnated with hope. This hope-vision is a gift from God to nourish, direct and delight his children. Like food, and like sunlight, it is a daily need. The one who has hope sees the kingdom being built, even when personal life might bring misfortune, sickness or oppression. Hope is eternal, whereas problems are of limited duration. Normal Christian life includes praying to God daily for replenished hope. It asks him to shed light on the tasks, small or large, that should be done for him.

Vision through hope also shows Christ. It sees beyond the Old Testament covenant of promise, to the covenant of Christ's presence. Our vision grows to become a vision with Christ. It grows when the light of heaven shows what we should do now. It sees that Jesus is with us. Vision in hope always recognises that God has come to us, and has made his home with us. Hope is not only in the spectacular, but also in things ordinary and mundane. Jesus is with us in daily activities, which take up the majority of time in normal Christian life.

Jesus and Revelation

The central awareness in the New Testament is one that is so obvious, it can easily be overlooked. It concerns the realisation and full implication of who Jesus is. Jesus is not merely a channel for God's law, or a prophet who shares with us what God wants us to hear, or a patriarch of the covenant. He is the revelation of God because he is God. Jesus is God, illuminated as never before!

His living presence is with us and in us, his Church. It is a gift beyond measure. In Christ is the fullness of God's revelation[4] and the fullness of his truth and love.

We, as Christ's followers, don't merely try to follow Christ's teaching when we want to follow God; we actually follow him. And we don't do this by staring at the heels of his sandals as he goes on ahead, but by sharing his own forward-looking vision. His view becomes that of his followers. He not only becomes the model for all, but his spirit must fill each of his followers. We must each be united, not only with the wisdom he shares, but with him, himself.

Vision and Christ's Light

In the New Testament there are many texts that speak of Jesus specifically as light.[5] The most notable of these is the prologue of John's gospel. Jesus is the light of goodness, which cannot be overshadowed by the darkness of evil.

In Matthew's gospel there is a statement that those who follow him should not only live in this light, but also be light. Each follower of Christ should let their own light shine before others ('Let your light so shine before men' Mt 5:16), so that personal witness to the light of Christ may become the light for others.

The light of God's revelation is found in its fullness in the person of Jesus. In the Old Testament, the best that could be managed was a set of laws and prophets. In the New Testament, the vision and understanding of God's will come through the person of Christ. They come through his teaching and through his example. I am to shine with Christ's light in me. I am offered, not merely a rule book, but a person to get to know. That is how my understanding of, and energy for, God's will can be deepened, by knowing Christ better.

Two starting-points, then, in the quest to see and do God's will are the gift of hope and the focus on Christ. To commence elsewhere is to begin without light. To start with hope and the true vision of Christ is to begin in the light. Hope and the presence of Christ in our daily lives offer both a vision of God's will and the energy to make his will, and his tasks, our own.

This first chapter considers 'hope' and 'focus on Christ' as the starting-points from which to see and do God's will.

NOTES

1.   I am grateful to Fr Ernest Ruch OMI, for telling the story at 'Lumen Christi' prayer group in Rome in 1993 or thereabouts.

2.   Psalms are quoted from the Grail translation, Collins 1963, London. All other scripture quotes in this book are from the RSV translation, Catholic Edition, CTS, London 1966.

3.   Examples of walking by God's light are also found in the New Testament, for example, Jn 8:12, 12:35; Eph 5:8; 1 Jn 1:7; Rev 21:24.

4.   See, for a clear explanation of this: John of the Cross, *The Ascent of Mount Carmel*, Book 2, Chap. 22. 3-5 found in the Office of Readings, Advent Week 2, Monday.

5.   Examples are: Mt 4:16; Lk 2:32; Jn 1, 3:19, 8:12, 9:5, 12:35; Eph 5; 1 Th 5:5; 1 Pet 2:9.

2

RELATIONSHIP WITH GOD

St Isidore of Seville, born about the year AD 560 in Spain, was a bishop and writer in the early Church. He linked the knowledge of God both to prayer and to reading of the scriptures.

> Prayer purifies us, reading instructs us. Both are good when both are possible. Otherwise prayer is better than reading. If a man wants to be in God's company, he must pray regularly and read regularly. When we pray we talk to God; when we read God talks to us.[1]

The Bible is the word of God. We read the scriptures to hear God's word. Our relationship with God deepens as we read. The scriptures are a normal companion to prayer in a Christian's daily life. All who seek God need nourishment and guidance from the scriptures. They are an integral part of our relationship with God in Christ.

But to whom is God speaking through scripture? To all of us, whatever age we are, and wherever we are on our spiritual journey. Each Christian grows or regresses in Christian life, seen in terms of their relationship with God in Christ. I am not at the same stage of faith now as I was ten years ago, nor at the stage where I will be in ten years time.

Have Some Madeira . . .

In their 'classic' recording 'At the Drop of a Hat', Michael Flanders and Donald Swann had a song about a seduction. Its chorus began, 'Have some Madeira, M'dear . . .' To most who listened to the song, the story and the moral were clear enough.[2]

One day it was sung to a young niece of the composer, who thought that she'd grasped what it was about. Her uncle's questioning, however, proved that there was one element which she'd misunderstood. Instead of realising that the cautionary tale was about alcohol, she surmised that the 'Madeira' warned against was Madeira cake!

Such confusion of 'Madeira wine' with 'Madeira cake' shows that the hearer has a different background to the one telling the story.

In a similar manner, it is easy to misinterpret scripture. Not only can words be misunderstood, but our understanding of them can be coloured by our own experience, the faith journey we have travelled and our life history.

The word of scripture speaks to Christians who have recently come to the faith, to those who are advanced on the path of personal commitment, and to the saints who are most close to God. Each person can develop or regress in their relationship with God. This can affect our use and perception of scripture.

Some passages of scripture may express a message in a way that has a particular, personal relevance to the individual at any given time. All passages of scripture can lead to God, but usually, at any moment, some passages seem to better inspire one person, and some another. This may be linked with a person's own spiritual journey and relationship with God.

Origen's Model

The three-men model, in the story of the cathedral builders, shows a difference in vision and understanding. This has a parallel in the insights of one of the first Christian writers on scripture, Origen (AD 185-254). In his 'Commentary on the Song of Songs',[3] he shares his vision of three stages of Christian growth in maturity, what we might call today a 'Journey in Faith'. Like the cathedral builders, he uses it to show a difference in people's understanding. Origen links each of his three stages of the Christian journey to one of the biblical books attributed to Solomon: i. Proverbs; ii. Ecclesiastes; and iii. The Song of Songs.

Some of Origen's ideas can be summarised as follows:

i. Proverbs compare simple alternatives, or give a simple moral directive. Many proverbs show a choice between two alternatives. One of them is portrayed as wise, true or good, and the other is shown to be flawed, or lacking in some respect. Origen knows that Christian growth often starts in wanting to reject sin. In this first stage there is need of moral teaching of the type found in Proverbs. Individuals need to know what offends God (sin) during the first phase of their relationship with him. There is a need to focus on what is revealed as right and wrong, and, with God's help, to be rid of sin and live in grace.

ii. The second book, Ecclesiastes, starts surprisingly by listing the things that people strive for in this world, and then saying 'all is vanity'. There comes a realisation that all things of the earth are temporary, and a better vision is that of the kingdom of heaven, which has no end. We are encouraged to see events in this world in relation to God. Sin is still fought and moral norms are kept, but most attention is directed beyond this. In this second stage of maturity[3] or spiritual development there is a growing awareness of the mystery of the Kingdom of God. It is a stage where the relationship deepens as more is seen of the mystery of God. We understand more of his creation, and of his personal call.

iii. The third book, The Song of Songs (or Song of Solomon), is a love poem. Time and again, attention is drawn to the different ways in which a human person expresses love, behaves when in love, and lives for the beloved and no one else. The call is that each person's relationship with God should grow to be like this. Still present is the revulsion when confronted by sin. More present is the vision beyond sin, looking towards the mystery of the Kingdom of God, but most present is the total 'being in love' with God. The deepest mystery in which to become engulfed is that of God's love for me, and my ever-failing, but never-despairing, attempts to reflect love in return. Each of us is to love God as a beloved loves the lover. God is my beloved.

Origen describes the first focus as 'moral'. The second he describes as 'natural'. The third, he calls 'contemplative'. In this final stage the love of the bride for the heavenly bridegroom is the model for the love of the perfect soul for God.

Not all of what Origen wrote was wise, or accepted by the Church,[4] but this particular model has stood the test of time well. Many Christian spiritual writers have used it or similar models to try to explain development and change as the Christian heart grows closer to God. The three-stage model has had various names. In the Middle Ages there were two common descriptions of a Christian's three-stage faith journey. One referred to the stages as beginners, proficients and perfects. The other described them in terms of a purgative way, an illuminative way and a unitive way. The model has been used by many writers and it is still useful today.

Origen's insights can also help us to understand that the Christian spiritual life should be one of growth. It is normal for a Christian's preoccupation to be with different aspects of the spiritual life at different times. Origen's ideas give an indication of why being forgiven, and being rid of sin, might be a focus of attention at some stages, why some aspect of the mystery of God might be most important at another stage, and why growing in love with God might loom large at some other time. The stages are not exclusive, however, nor is there an assumption that each person will always move from one to another with time. At any time one focus or understanding might predominate in a Christian's life, though usually the other two aspects will also be present, playing a lesser role.

Reading or listening to scripture, and reflecting on it, is essential. It is better to read, however, with some knowledge and understanding. The devil is portrayed as able to quote scripture in his attempts to bring about evil rather than good (Mt 4:3-9). Origen is not seeking to encourage a restricted reading of scripture, which would make it easier for the devil to work such tricks. Although Origen singles out different books of scripture to represent individual stages of Christian growth, this does not mean that we should limit our reflections to one book of scripture at a time. The reverse is true. A broad knowledge and understanding of scripture is of more use, and more secure, than a narrow use. Without a wide background we may easily misinterpret, be misled, and mislead ourselves, using inappropriate passages of scripture.

This chapter introduces a model of stages of growth in the spiritual life, and looks at our use of the scriptures to help us as we make Christian choices.

NOTES

1.   From *The Book of Maxims,* in the Office of Readings for the proper of the feast of St Isidore, 4 April (Boston: St Paul Editions, 1983).
2.   Too much Madeira led to a young lady's downfall.
3.   Origen, 'Prologue to the Commentary on Song of Songs', in *Origen,* trans. Rowan A. Greer. Classics of Western Spirituality Series (New York: Paulist Press, 1979), pp. 217-44.
4.   Some of Origen's other teaching was later condemned by the Church, but his models given here have been widely found useful and do not conflict with sound teaching.

3

PERSONAL STAGES OF FAITH AND CHOICE

When a Christian seeks to choose what is good, a three-stage (or three-level) model may also be used to represent the nature of the selection that is made. The term 'discernment of spirits' is sometimes used to indicate a choice made by a Christian for, or against, God.

'Discernment' in the English language has several common meanings. It can suggest 'seeing' or 'evaluating' or 'distinguishing', or a combination of these. (The meanings of 'discernment', particularly in scripture, are discussed later in this book.[1])

Spiritual discernment, in terms of seeing and making distinctions, can be described on three levels, too, as in the following scheme suggested by Michael Buckley[2]:

The first distinction in 'discernment of spirits' might be portrayed as the choice between the 'flesh' and the 'spirit' (Gal 5:19-21; Rom 13:12). 'Flesh' here encompasses those things that are selfish and self-centred, and 'spirit' refers to the alternatives. This is a simple moral distinction between things that are of their nature good or bad. Some choice (i.e. some Christian discernment) is to do simply with making a moral decision. An example of this type of decision would be the choice to end a quarrel by peacemaking (Gal 5:22 'The fruit of the spirit is peace, joy . . .' etc.).

The second distinction can be seen in the commitment to 'Jesus as Lord' ('No one can say "Jesus is Lord", except by the Holy Spirit' [1 Cor 12:3]). Here, the mystery of God, shown in Jesus and salvation history, is the key. Those who make decisions guided by their insight into these mysteries, make different choices from those who are guided by other considerations. Some choice, or some Christian discernment, is in the realm of the understanding of Jesus and the bringing about of our salvation. An example of this might be where in a time of distress, or severe trial, someone who would not have called themselves either Christian or prayerful, has the experience that 'God comes in',[3] enabling them to perceive that he, in person, had been there all the time.

The third distinction can be described in terms of those who live in the Spirit and are guided by it (Gal 5:16, 18) and are seen as children of God (Rom 8:14). This implies a union with God on a more intimate level, and is not unlike Origen's third model, of bridal imagery. It represents the ideal goal in a Christian's relationship with God. Some choice, or some Christian discernment, takes place in the realm of this personal intimacy with God. Here I am reminded, among others, of Blessed Dominic Barberi (a nineteenth-century Italian priest who came to preach in England). It is said that on being stoned when walking through a village in Staffordshire, he picked up a stone, kissed it and put it in his pocket.[4] What better witness of intimate union with the suffering Christ could he have made? and yet by any other reckoning it seems bizarre.

The use of such categorisation, though it can be supported by scriptural texts, may seem to make too much use of 'categories'. The danger is that a personal relationship with God is reduced to a 'type'. In truth, I am not a 'type' of Christian any more than a child can be seen as a 'type' of son or daughter. Categories must be used with caution, and yet there is something useful in them, as they help to explain many different experiences in a way that gives an overall picture of God's love. They link God's calling, and human response and growth, to the different appreciation and use of scripture that may be found by those who read or hear it. They give an inkling of why the choices that the great saints view as important (whether it be St Francis of Assisi, choosing poverty,[5] or St Thérèse of Lisieux, choosing her little way[6]) may be different from those choices that others, less intimate with God, see as being significant.

Reflecting on Scriptures when Trying to Make Choices

Any personal selection of the scriptures can easily colour the interpretation of 'God's will' that scripture contains. For anyone who is familiar with even a portion of the scriptures it is easy to know which books contain topics of condemnation, which of praise, which of reliance on God, which of courage and so on. What is to stop me, or anyone, consciously or otherwise, looking at one passage when seeking affirmation, and another when looking for condemnation? Self-deception then becomes more likely . . . by simply finding a text of scripture that upholds any view (whether sound or prejudiced) rather than my being formed by scripture as a whole.

The Spirit's gifts of wisdom and understanding are given to the body of the Church to help each person as part of that body. It is helpful to know the context in which the particular Bible passages were written and have been interpreted by the Church. Interpretation and discernment are more sure in this broad context than when carried out in a 'go it alone' approach with a narrow scriptural frame of reference. It is also important to raise up both the heart and the mind (to use not only feelings, but also intelligence) in prayer for God's guidance when using scriptures.

There are two points worth remembering when using the scriptures to help to recognise and do God's will:

> i. There are basic moral teachings in some books of scripture. A growing relationship with God will take us deeper than simply seeing him in moral terms. Any inspiration that clearly contradicts these moral precepts, however, should be viewed with great caution.

> ii. It is better to have a broad knowledge and consideration of scripture than a narrow one when praying for and seeking God's will. It is wise to see how the Church interprets scriptures, in addition to using personal

reflections. Neither intellect nor emotions should be ignored during prayer and reflection on scriptures.

This chapter relates the state of a Christian's relationship with God with the choices which that person presumes they are called to make. It is normal that different aspects of spiritual life seem important at different times on our spiritual journey, so different types of choice may be most important as the Christian life progresses. Sacred scripture is one of the prime means by which God speaks and leads us, whatever the nature of our relationship with him. Individuals may be helped to make a good choice by using diverse passages of scripture. A wide knowledge of, and reflection on the scriptures as a whole, is encouraged.

NOTES

1. See Chapter 9.
2. See Michael J. Buckley, SJ, 'Discernment of Spirits', in *The New Dictionary of Catholic Spirituality*, ed. Michael Downey (Collegeville, Minnesota: The Liturgical Press, 1993), p. 276.
3. This phrase was used by Joy Gresham (who was later to marry C. S. Lewis), when her husband, Bill, phoned to say he had a mental breakdown, leaving her in turmoil. See Humphrey Carpenter, *The Inklings* (London: Harper Collins, 1997), p. 236.
4. I haven't seen this in print, so I can't vouch for its authenticity. Regardless of historicity, however, this gives an indication of the type of action that falls into this category.
5. For example: 'I, brother Francis, the little one, wish to follow the life and poverty of our most high lord Jesus Christ and of his most holy mother and to persevere in this until the end' from Francis's 'Last Will Written for St Clare

and her sisters', in *Francis and Clare, The Complete Works,* eds. R. J. Armstrong and I. C. Brady, Classics of Western Spirituality Series (New York: Paulist Press, 1982), p. 46.

6. See *St Thérèse of Lisieux: Autobiography of a Saint,* trans. Ronald Knox (Harper Collins/Fount Classics, 1977).

4

PRAYER, LISTENING, AND CHOICE

Making the Decisions

Recently I traded-in my car. It had proved more expensive than I hoped in service costs over the last year. I had a week or two when I wasn't too busy, in which I could concentrate on it. I wouldn't want to change it precipitously, or when dozens of other things were also on my mind.

For me, choosing a car is not easy. It requires me to invest money in the result of a decision that may be flawed or may later be shown to have been foolish. There always seems to be too many factors to take into account. How much should I spend? What is available? How can I tell if it's suitable? Will it give good value for money? Will the compromises between size, acceleration, comfort, economy and so on work out happily?

At the same time there is something pleasing about exercising my individual choice in an act of some (financial) consequence.

I spent some days looking through motor magazines and want-ads. I visited car showrooms, mostly indulging my fancies and fantasies, but in doing so I realised that many of my dream machines had roofs that were too low and would not have been suitable. Next I phoned insurance companies, looked at running costs and tried to assess what I would be contented to drive for the next few years.

Finally I came to a realisation of what I felt was best. I drew up a list which looked something like this:

> New car must
> have enough headroom
> and comfort
> be group 8 insurance or less
> do over thirty-five miles per gallon

ideally have done less than 50,000 miles
ideally be a hatchback
ideally cost no more than £2000 to trade-up
ideally be part of a part-exchange deal.

I went back round the car showrooms and, within two further days, asked for and found the best car available, and committed myself to it. I was glad that it seemed to fit well the criteria I had listed. Like much in life it was a practical business, with hopes that gradually built up and came to fruition.

The process could be seen in three parts: first, recognising the 'time to do something'; second, realising what 'seems to be wanted', and third, asking around to see what is available. Choosing a car is something that is relatively trivial. Christian decisions may be about trivia, but are often about how to spend our lives, not simply about spending our money.

Sometimes the relationship of prayer with decisions of Christian life may have a similar sequence. First in prayer comes the intuition that there is a decision to be made, or a new direction to be taken. Second is the time of listening (whilst using all faculties to clarify what to ask for), and third the asking for what is needed. As with the car, personal free will is important.

Jesus, Prayer and Decisions

Before making decisions, and before he suffered, Jesus spent much time in prayer. For example, he prayed all night before choosing the apostles (Lk 6:12), he prayed before his passion and death (Mt 26: 36-39). The starting point for the early followers of Jesus, too, was to spend much time in prayer before making important decisions or choices, for example, Acts 1:12-26, where prayer was integral in the selection of Matthias as an apostle (also see Acts 4:31, 6:6). Time spent in prayer is vital in order to make good decisions, or to understand God's will. Neither is it enough to give only a few cursory moments to prayer, nor must it be automatic. Jesus, in praying all night before a major decision, gave an example, not to be reduced, by us, to praying for only a few minutes.

It is often only when the first grace has been given (i.e., realising in prayer that 'now is the time' for something) that I pause and question how I should follow this up.

So what are we to do in prayer when decisions are to be made? Three types of prayer associated with choosing to follow God are:

    i.   Prayer reflecting on current life.
    ii. Prayer that listens to God
    iii. Prayer that asks God.

As we undertake each of these seriously, more is learned about the making of choices, and about that power to bring good things into effect, which God may choose to share between himself and the one who prays.

Listening in Prayer
Elijah Listening to God (1 Kings 19:9-18)

A good example of listening in prayer is seen in Elijah's encounter with God in the cave on Mount Horeb. God told Elijah that he wanted him to come to Mount Horeb. Elijah responded and came. Elijah was on the mountain when there was hurricane, earthquake and fire, but realised that God was not present in any of them. Only when there came the sound of a gentle breeze, did Elijah come to the mouth of the cave to listen for God. When he listened in the silence he heard God explaining what he was to do next.

Perhaps finding God in silence was not what Elijah envisaged. He might reasonably have expected to find God in more powerful signs. Only when these had run their course did he realise that God was to be found in silence. This knowledge can be a support to us when the 'time of power' seems to have run out without God speaking.

It is also a reminder of the need for quiet listening in prayer when decisions or choices have to be made. The need for attentive prayer in silence in order to hear God's word has often been stressed by Christian spiritual writers.

A mid-fifth-century bishop, Diadochus of Photice, wrote a treatise on spiritual perfection,[1] in which discernment is a major topic. He suggests that the mind should be capable of distinguishing good and bad choices presented to it, just as it can tell dark from light. When this doesn't happen, he suggests the reason is often anxiety. He states that the ability to maintain a tranquil mind, even in the midst of troubles, is an important key in listening to God. Stillness (hesychia) has been praised for many centuries, particularly in the Eastern Churches, as an important part of the Christian's way to God.

Asking God in Prayer
David and the illness of Bathsheba's child (2 Sam 12:15 ff)
Another process of growing to know and accept God's will is shown by David, when Bathsheba's child was ill. In this instance, unlike Elijah, David started with a fixed idea of what he wanted God's will to be. What went on was not the obvious making of a choice, nor listening, but the example is relevant nevertheless. David strongly expressed a personal wish that the child should live. He fasted and slept on sacking on the ground. He pleaded with God for the child's life. But when the child died, he conceded that this was God's will, as if satisfied that he'd done all he could by his own efforts, but accepting the outcome nonetheless. He knew that he had done his best. He accepted God's will. He then arose, washed and took food.

Many who pray find it easy to be in sympathy with this last account. Often it is only when a particular outcome to a situation has been prayed for, and all that can be thought of has been done, that we are at peace when something happens other than that for which we had prayed. On other occasions, when there has been no effort in prayer, there is less acceptance that a different outcome is the will of God. (In secular human terms, the same experience holds too. Sometimes it's only after seriously yearning for a Mercedes that I realise a lesser car is better for me!)

The story of David and the child shows that the understanding of God's will, and the gaining of courage to accept it, may come from a process that starts as intercessory or petitionary prayer. It is a reminder of the integral link that exists between prayer and discernment.

Often discernment and prayer of petition are very closely linked, either when they together bring about that which is hoped for by the one who prays (e.g., Lazarus rising from the dead when Jesus prays, Jn 11) or, with David, where this doesn't happen.

Both listening and asking are normal in Christian prayer.

Power, Will and Freedom
In addition to the final acceptance of God's will, David clearly showed his own will and freedom. He also used the spiritual power of prayer and fasting. Four elements were at work here:

   i.   God's will.
   ii. Human will.
   iii. Spiritual power.
   iv. Freedom.

The mystery of the interaction of these four elements accepts that both God and humans have freedom, and both God and humans have spiritual power. The Christian call is to put personal freedom and power at God's service. We are called not to ignore them, but to use them with God. Taking discernment seriously involves entering into the mystery of these four elements. When we pray to be guided by God, there could be several outcomes:

i. That for which we pray, may happen. God wants the effect of prayer to bring about the good for which we pray.

ii. We may become aware of God's will, either by events, or by some form of revelation, or through some particular method of prayer and reflection that we use to help us to make a choice.

iii. We may not seem to have any greater understanding of God's specific will for the choice we have to make, but still may be strengthened to pursue one particular aspect of self-giving generosity, or virtue.

iv. We may not end up with a conviction to follow any particular course of action, but may be strengthened in some commitment to prayer or ascetic discipline (e.g. fasting with prayer, like David), knowing that often prayer and other disciplines can bring about good in the world, or make choices clearer.

v. We may have to grapple with the freedom that God has given each of us, or we may grapple with accepting God's own freedom to bring about whatever he wills or allows.

This chapter gives reflections on some aspects of prayer and of personal free will and choice, and provides a introduction to the interrelation between them.

NOTES

1. The section on discernment from this letter can be found in the Office of Readings for Wednesday in the fourth week of the Church's year (also Migne **PG 65**, 1169, 1175-1176).

5

NORMS OF LIFE AND NORMS OF ACTION

One story[1] about Mother Teresa of Calcutta often comes to my mind and I find it helpful for reflection. It tells of the time when she was first convinced that God wanted her to help those who were dying on the Calcutta streets.

Mother Teresa encountered much opposition. There were many whom she wanted to help, but she had few resources. Some people of influence in the city thought it a pipe-dream; that she wouldn't be able to do anything useful. It is said that one of them challenged her on this, 'There are thousands of destitute people dying in the city, how are you going to help them?' Her reply was disarming. She simply said, 'One at a time.'

I am impressed for two reasons. First, because of the simplicity of her response. Second, because she didn't linger to question the means, nor avoid taking personal responsibility to do something about those in need. The simplicity is related to the clarity of her understanding . . . if people are dying in inhuman conditions . . . God wants something done about it . . . start with the first one!

In her position, would I respond in the same way? My suspicion is that I would delay taking any action. I might even use some form of prayer or spiritual exercise as an excuse to postpone starting on such a mammoth task. She didn't. She was prompt to act with practical love.

Prayer and use of scripture do require time and a focus of attention and energy. These must be given regularly and generously in our lives. If too great a focus is given exclusively to these, however, then our energies might be distracted from *doing* good by too much time being spent *deciding* what is good. Time can be spent on reflection which should be spent witnessing by action to Christian love. Much Christian action can be governed

31

by norms and guidelines that have been revealed in scripture and developed in the Church.

Some such guidelines are as follows:

The Spiritual Gifts Mentioned in the Old Testament

In the scriptures we see that God provides gifts to help his people to carry out actions that are in accord with his will. Although discernment is not often mentioned in the Hebrew scriptures, other gifts do feature. The best known of these are wisdom, understanding, counsel, fortitude, knowledge, piety and fear of the Lord (Isa 11:2-3). These are often seen as the Old Testament gifts of the Spirit. Other gifts and virtues are also encouraged, such as justice (e.g. Ex 23:1-3, Ps 81:1-4), honesty (e.g. Job 6:25), faithfulness (e.g. 1 Sam 2:9, 26:23; Ps 100:6), and integrity (e.g. 1 Kings 9:4). In Isaiah we also find the promise of the gift of righteousness (Isa 11:5). From the book of Daniel are promised wisdom and knowledge (Dan 2:20-22).

All these scripture texts remind us of the many different supports God gives to his people. He leads us not only by a direct call, but also by many gifts and talents which enable us to be aware of, to choose, and to do what is good.

Personal Conviction

Actions or choices often come from our personal convictions of what is right or good, and what God's will requires. Motivations that influence such choices are described using various words. Sometimes general terms best sum up what guides us: conscience, virtue, wisdom, as well as morals, ethics, goodness, right, and so on.

Particular terms such as the traditional specific virtues (fortitude, fidelity, prudence, and others) also play a part. So when we talk of 'searching conscience', 'being kind', 'trying to help someone', 'living a virtuous life', or 'asking God for wisdom', we acknowledge influences and ideas that direct Christian life and loving actions towards God's will.

In an immediate sense this is not discernment, nor necessarily to do with consciously making choices. In an ongoing and important way, however, it is. Indeed, any action filled with God's love, or prompted by it, is an action according to his will.

Norms of the Church

In the tradition of the Church there is a set of norms that ideally should become instinctive behaviour. They are based on precepts of the Old and New Testament scriptures (e.g. Tob 12, Isa 58, Mt 5:3-10, Mt 25). They include norms of helping people spiritually (spiritual works of mercy) and norms of helping them in simple humanitarian ways (corporal works of mercy).

Spiritual Works of Mercy
1. To convert the sinner; 2. To instruct the ignorant; 3. To counsel the doubtful; 4. To comfort the sorrowful; 5. To bear wrongs patiently; 6. To forgive injuries; 7. To pray for the living and the dead.

Corporal Works of Mercy
1. To feed the hungry; 2. To give drink to the thirsty; 3. To clothe the naked; 4. To shelter the homeless; 5. To visit the sick; 6. To visit the imprisoned; 7. To bury the dead.

No Good Alternative

Often circumstances of life show where there is a good to be done, and no major alternative good is on the cards. There is simply no need of a process of discernment when there is no real choice; it doesn't enter the picture (though courage may still be needed). Doing an obvious good is doing the will of God. Ignoring an obvious good, when there are no alternatives (which are good) on offer, is to ignore God's will. It is only when there is a choice of actions, both of which seem good, that some process of discernment is needed.

Two important virtues, associated with openness to God, are humility and familiarity.

Humility

As has already been mentioned, many writers make a link between the ability to be still, or to listen, and the facility of good discernment.[2] This link is made strongly, not only in the scriptures, but also by early Christian monastic communities. This type of stillness or openness to God is often associated with the virtue of humility.

In the early Eastern Christian Church, a Greek monk, John Climacus (579-649), shared this view.[3] One image which he gives is that of the lemon tree. He describes the lemon tree as able to stand upright with branches directed to the sky, until the time comes to bear fruit. He notes that when the tree is bearing fruit, its branches must, of their nature, bow down.[4] Any gift that comes from God, or any good spirit, will lead to the fruit of the Spirit being evident. The image of the tree bearing fruit, and being bowed down in humility as it does so, gives the image for discernment. As discernment is authentic, so it is fruitful. As it is fruitful, so it is linked with humility.

The scriptures, too, show God giving his grace, or letting his power work through the humble (e.g. Jas 4:6, 1 Pet 5:5, and perhaps most clearly with Mary, in Lk 1). To discern, we must be open. To be open, we must be humble. Without humility, God can't get through.

From the later period of Christianity, Ignatius of Loyola (1491-1556) is a key writer in the Western Christian Church on discernment. He includes reflections on the benefits of humility, the need for it, and the types of humility, in the first week of his spiritual exercises.[5] Ignatius sees humility in three stages:

i. To be humble in subjecting our lives to God's law.

ii. To humble ourselves to the point where we are indifferent whether we are rich or poor, honoured or despised, long or short-lived, but only care to serve God as well as possible.

iii. To seek Christ-like humility, having poverty as Christ was poor, being insulted as Christ was insulted, so that there is an affiliation to Christ in the way we are treated in this world.

The need for humility, and the association of this virtue with good discernment, is as strong today as it has ever been. Most good reflections on humility by spiritual writers take us beyond the popular secular vision of being humble, which can often imply lacking courage, to a Christ-centred humility that requires a strong sacrificial courage inspired by him. The paradox of humility is that it requires us to become both weaker and stronger: we become weaker in wanting our own selfish way, but much stronger in submitting to God's way.

Familiarity

One monk in the early Church with much experience of monastic communities in the East, was John Cassian. He lived in the late fourth and early fifth centuries, and when he finally settled in France, he became an adviser to the new monasteries in Europe on various aspects of spiritual life. Among his writings is a conference on discernment,[6] in which he insists that both humility and familiarity with things of God must be present in order for discernment to take place.

He has a particularly good image of the need for familiarity with God and all the things of God. He likens the gift of discernment to the ability of money-changers to know whether a coin that bears the imprint of a king's head is authentic or a forgery. It is a comparison that means a lot to me personally, because of my own lack of such skill.

Early last year I was walking with a friend in the hills of Shropshire, and we called at a country pub for lunch. I offered the barmaid a £20 note from my wallet to pay for the meals. She scrutinised it carefully, and gave it back to me, saying she thought it might be a forgery, as the Queen's nose on the watermark seemed too large. I wasn't convinced, but as I had no other Queen's noses with which to compare it, I didn't argue the point. On my return home I mentioned the note to someone who had previously worked in a bank, and I showed it to him. Martin didn't examine the note at all, merely took it from me, immediately gave it back and said, 'Yes, it's a forgery. It's the wrong paper.'

I felt in the presence of a professional! In my mind I remembered the barmaid, measuring Queen's noses, and myself, with even less knowledge, seeing nothing unusual. Here was a man who'd had many thousands of notes through his hands, and knew just by the feel that it was a fake. I tried and failed to think of any better person to judge the note's authenticity. No book-knowledge or intelligence could surpass it. No position of authority would lead to more certain identification. Simple familiarity, and working with the currency, is the key to spotting a forgery.

Perhaps Cassian had the same experience, perhaps not. What is sure is that he saw a similarity between the skills of money-handlers and those of people who seek to discern. Cassian recognises several aspects of the ability to appreciate things of God, that of it being a gift, and that of it being an ability, associated with experience, with understanding and with knowledge. He does so by asking this important discernment question, 'How well do you recognise the likeness of God?', and he uses the coin as a symbol in this question. Like so many choices we make each day, clarity is often lacking: I rarely choose between two courses of action that seem to be in 'mint condition'. Likewise, often even the poorest 'forgery', in order to deceive me, has some likeness to the monarch in its image.

When the analogy is examined, the implications for Christian choice are clear. What becomes important in discernment is not specifically some learned knowledge, nor a particular skill or dexterity, but the innate power to recognise him whom we should love most (i.e. God). Each small characteristic of God contributes to his image. It is not enough to say a monarch has a small nose, because on any particular coin the nose may not be clear, just like meeting a friend who wears a scarf, partially hiding their face, shouldn't cause anyone who knows them well to doubt their identity.

Cassian's model implies, above all, that our recognising of God, and things of God, improves as we love God more than anyone or anything else; when we know him, not selectively through *either* scriptures, *or* prayer, *or* his body the Church, *or* the sacraments, *or* the truth revealed about God through revelation, *or* in the marginalised and suffering,[7] but through *all* of them. This gift is not distinct from the totality of a person's life being turned towards God, but rather builds upon that total commitment and dedication.

The Eastern writer John Climacus has other good ideas to share. His further reflections on discernment put it in an even wider framework, which includes the sacrament of baptism. He draws together several different aspects of the spiritual life. When he talks of Christian perception, he sees it as a property of the soul which comes from conscience. Conscience, for him, is the guidance (word and censure) of our guardian angel[8] from baptism.

We, too, should reflect on our sacramental baptism, as our own starting-point for discernment. Indeed, the whole sacramental life of the Church immerses its members in Christ, and we are nourished and strengthened by all the sacraments.

John Climacus says also that discernment combines an incorrupt conscience with a purity of perception, and that it is found only in those who are themselves pure in heart, body and speech. Many of his ideas, and those of Cassian, Ignatius and other spiritual writers, come down to the same challenge that can be found in the scriptures, a challenge to grow in personal holiness, without which there will always be a block to the full and fruitful knowing and doing of God's will.

This chapter is a reminder of the importance of general actions and virtues, in keeping with God's will. Four sets of guidelines (spiritual gifts, personal conviction, norms of the Church, and no good alternative) and two important virtues (humility and familiarity) are discussed. Living the virtues and using norms and guidelines can promote immediate Christian response, enabling us to do what God wants. They may help us to avoid dithering, which may otherwise be present, sometimes disguised, as prayer or spiritual exercises.

NOTES

1. I haven't seen this story in print, so can't give documentary evidence for its authenticity.
2. Chapter 4, note 1.
3. John Climacus, *The Ladder of Divine Ascent*, trans. Colum Luibheid and Norman Russell. Classics of Western Spirituality Series (New York: Paulist Press, 1982), chap. 25, p. 228.
4. John Climacus, *The Ladder of Divine Ascent*, chap. 25, p. 225.
5. Ignatius of Loyola *Spiritual Exercises*, English translation by Louis Puhl SJ (Chicago: Loyola University Press, 1955), Exercises 164-9.
6. John Cassian, 'Conference Two', in *Conferences*, trans. Colm Luibheid, Classics of Western Spirituality Series (New York: Paulist Press, 1985), pp. 60-81.
7. Mt 25:40-45 ('whenever you do this to the least . . .').
8. John Climacus, *The Ladder of Divine Ascent*, Step 26, p. 260.

6

CHOOSING WITH GOD IN THE OLD TESTAMENT AND IN THE NEW

Old Testament Reflections

i. Gideon and the Fleece (Judg 6:37-40)

In the book of Judges, Gideon, apparently seeking God's will, asked God for a sign: that a fleece might be covered with dew and the ground not covered, and then vice-versa. He asked for this in order that he might know whether God would use him to deliver Israel from their enemies. God obliged and provided Gideon with the signs. The process seemed to work . . . but at the same time it is far from ideal. A more detailed look at Gideon's situation reveals why.

Earlier in the book of Judges (6:11-32) God seemed to have spoken clearly to Gideon, using a messenger who gave Gideon a sign of fire, which consumed meat and cakes (6:20-22). Gideon accepted that this earlier sign confirmed the message that he (Gideon) would 'rescue Israel from Midian's hand'(6:14).

So the later incident of the fleece was not about a genuine doubt of Gideon concerning what God wanted or had told Gideon to do. The real question was not about God's will, but about Gideon's courage. In this instance God did respond to Gideon's request. In doing so he supported and built up Gideon's confidence.

We might be tempted to criticise Gideon's procedures as putting God to the test, but this is not necessarily the case. What is shown is twofold. First, that there is a human frailty which, when courage is put to the test, may play the game of 'seeking discernment', when what is really lacking is confidence or courage. But second, that God treats us as his beloved children, and even when presented with a masquerade of this sort, may choose to support and lead us, rather than sternly criticise us for testing him.

ii. The false comforters in the book of Job (Job 4-28)
A further example of false discernment can be found in the book of Job. In the course of that book, various arguments were put to Job, by his companions, to explain his misfortunes. These included the false judging (false discerning) that his misfortunes were a sign from God that Job had done something wrong. Job honestly protested his good character and actions, refusing to be led into his companions' way of thinking. He was right in his attitude. Relying on 'signs' alone can easily lead to people ignoring the truth that is known through adherence to God's Law, witnessed in one's own life.

iii. Saul and the witch of Endor (1 Sam 28:6 ff)
After asking God unsuccessfully, Saul is pictured trying to find out things using dreams, divination, prophets, and then finally consulting a medium (the witch of Endor). Yes, Saul got what he wanted; his question was answered but it was not by a method that responded in love to God's power, or through anything good, that this information was given to him. (The witch conjured up the dead Samuel, who answered Saul's questions.) Nor was the information a blessing to Saul; it foretold defeat.

Simply wanting knowledge is not enough, nor is it always to be commended, if it is not accompanied by a desire for God's will and a desire to grow closer to God as one's questions are answered. Saul's process was not holy, not prayerful, not trusting in God, and was harmful rather than beneficial in his relationship with God. It shows that Saul was desperate, but does not give us a good example of discernment. It serves, rather, as a reminder that the end does not justify the means.

All of the above attempts, however, do witness to a need felt by the people of God to consult him about important choices, and they indicate that God sometimes clearly guides his people. But at other times his guidance isn't clear.

New Testament Reflections

i. Doing the master's will

Mt 21:28-32 (The parable of the two sons: one said he would do his father's will, but didn't; the other said he wouldn't do the father's will, but changed his mind and did it.)

Mt 25:14-30 (The parable of the talents: the master expects the servants to use their own judgement and business skills to increase the talents at their disposal.)

Lk 12:47 (The account of the servant who knows what the master wants, but does nothing and is punished when the master returns.)

Lk 19:11-27 (The parable of the pounds.)

Sometimes in the accounts in the gospels, the immediate precise understanding of the father's will is shown to be much less important than the final courage and determination to do what is good and right. So in the parables of the talents and the pounds, what is praised is the fidelity to the master's wishes, combined with personal initiative and drive to carry out the broad aims of his will.

Some people expend more energy trying to know God's will. Others put more effort into developing the courage and determination to do good. Neither by itself is sufficient; both direction and courage are needed. The passages suggest that when the day of judgement comes, the putting into action of something that is an obvious good will be judged to be of greater importance than the initial discernment. The parables of the talents and the pounds act as a strong reminder not to spend too much time procrastinating. But the doing of God's will can't be achieved without, at least in some measure, knowing what that will might be. A mature Christian must know that there is a job to be done, and then get on and do it.

The view that these parables give should encourage a spontaneity to say 'yes' to God in our own lives. The ideal response shown through the parables should become second nature to us. These New Testament texts indicate that there is now less need for specific discernment of what to do than in Old Testament days (as so much is revealed in Christ). This should enable more personal energy and courage to be put into tasks that will build up God's kingdom.

ii. Being unencumbered
(Lk 14:16-24, Mt 22:2-14)

Jesus tells a parable about a group of people who were invited to the master's banquet. They made excuses not to come. In Luke's account, one had bought land, one some oxen, and another had taken a wife. In Matthew's account, one went to his business, another to his farm, and others killed the master's messengers. The master then turned his attention away from these, his first-choice guests, and invited others, who were unencumbered by possessions or responsibilities, and who responded to the call.

Following reflection on such a parable, we might pray for the awareness of how possessions and responsibilities may close our ears to God's call to us. We can then make efforts to be as free as we can from attachments to them.

iii. Mary's discernment of God's will for her (Lk 1:26-56)

In Luke's gospel, when Mary receives the revelation made by an angel, she does not immediately understand what it is all about. Indeed, she is deeply disturbed, wonders what it might mean, and asks questions (Lk 1:28-35). Her consent to what follows is specifically a submission to God's will, and she accepts it as a servant or handmaid (Lk 1:37-38). Mary responds not only to a *call* (from God), but also then to a *need* (of Elizabeth). She goes to help her cousin. The first revelation from God, and Mary's response, is followed by a confirming leap of John the Baptist in Elizabeth's womb, and Elizabeth's interpretation of that leap (Lk 1:40-44). There follows an inspiring expression of joy in God's greatness, in total humility, as Mary proclaims the Magnificat (Lk 1: 46-56).

The overall sequence for Mary is:

i. Revelation, followed by

ii. personal reflection and questioning, then

iii. acceptance without conditions, then

iv. responding also (without being asked) to Elizabeth's human need ('Yes' to God, followed by 'Yes' to need), then

v. a confirmation of revelation by the words and actions of others, then

vi. a personal witness of Mary's humility, combined with

vii. a proclamation of God's greatness, and acknowledgement of his gifts.

There is a wholeness and integrity about the sequence that is well worth reflecting on, and asking that it be mirrored in our own discernment and acceptance of God's call.

iv. Jesus' testing in the desert (Mt 4, Lk 4, Mk 1:12-13)

A clear picture of the working of an evil spirit (Satan) is shown immediately after Jesus is baptised by John. In Matthew's account the three temptations are:

i. to satisfy hunger;

ii. to presume that angels will protect him when he does something that seems imprudent (suicidal?);

iii. to 'do a deal', where material power is to be had by doing homage to Satan.

How different these propositions are from the ones offered to Mary! There is no element of 'entering into an unknown mystery of God', which was present with Mary. There is an appeal to things that are portrayed as immediately self-satisfying. This compares with something that was likely to cause personal problems in Mary's case. (A girl found pregnant before marriage, by someone other than her prospective husband, could legally be stoned to death.)

Another odd aspect is the timing of the testing of Jesus, which follows an obvious grace (baptism) and is during a period of asceticism. Does baptism lead us into the mystery of God, which includes facing false attractions and recognising them as evil? The spirits that we should be wary of are those that seem to entice us to satisfy the body, to ignore virtue (e.g. prudence) or to be attracted to personal power when the means to obtain it are not in themselves holy. Perhaps the times when we should be most wary are those that follow obvious occasions of grace.

v. Peter's Mis-discernment (Mt 16:23, Mk 8:33)

When a friend has just indicated that he is to suffer and die at the hands of others, it seems not unreasonable to say, like Peter, 'This must not happen to you' (Mt 16:22). The reply, 'Get behind me, Satan', comes as a bit of a shock. The only explanation given by Jesus is that Peter is thinking 'not like God, but like a human being' (Mt 16:23).

What does this say about our attempts at discernment, where the first reaction is to try to avoid any human suffering or hardship? Discernment where there is suffering in store is not easy. Both compassion (perhaps involving looking for an end to suffering) and also seeking unity with Christ (even though this may include a cross) are instincts that may be present. A spontaneous human response may well be contrary to God. Initial reactions are often to avoid pain, renunciation and sacrifice at all costs.

It is often difficult to understand what God wants, or why he might allow suffering. Peter's reaction is mirrored in the instinctive response of many Christians in similar circumstances. We, too, may be part of a mystery of suffering that often seems obscure. Our initial reaction may often differ from that of Christ.

This chapter shows something of the variety and richness of scripture. It offers reflections on a few key texts. These indicate a diversity in the way that God guides his people and leads each of us. It is good to reflect on a wide range of texts and to be open to the many ways in which God might lead us.

7

PROPHETS, PROPHECY AND SIGNS FROM GOD

When travelling down unknown country roads I treat signposts with caution; I have gone down wrong roads too often. How easy it is for someone to turn the top of the post round, so that the sign that says 'Southam' points down a road running in the opposite direction. When in unfamiliar territory, however, signs can also be a boon. Prophets are the same; good ones are very helpful, but if they are turned from the true direction, or if false to start with, they cause confusion.

Covenant, Law and Prophecy

The Old Testament tells of the history of the relationship between God and his chosen people. This includes the covenant, which is accompanied by themes of prophecy and Law. The people accept the Law and try to follow it, and God leads them and cares for them. God reveals himself to them by Law and prophecy. The key to the people's response to such revelation is the twofold task of understanding and obeying Law, and recognising true and false prophets.

The prophet was seen as a gift to the community. In prophecy, he linked God to his people. Prophecy more usually focused on a community than on an individual. The prophet was firmly rooted in the traditions as well as the problems of the society. True prophets had a tremendous zeal, which made them speak out bravely against injustice, evil and all forms of straying from God. Part of this drive came from a deep love of the tradition. Prophets did not cast overboard the richness of the tradition, but rather renewed and refounded it. Some texts (e.g. Jer 23:14 ff and Deut 18:21) suggest that prophets were to be judged by their own orthodoxy, the fulfilment of their prophecy, the contents of their prophecy and the morality of their lives.

Prophecy was more often of doubtful authenticity when it concerned an individual rather than a community, when it made the prophet important or rich, when it gave people a 'pat on the back' rather than challenged them, when it harmed rather than renewed tradition. When the people of God heard prophecy, their ability to distinguish true from false depended on the living faith of the community, including its fidelity to, and sense of, the covenant (often seen in terms of Law).[1]

With any prophecy, pride and self-satisfaction can creep in. Not only can pride persuade people that they are holy when the opposite is true, but it can also persuade them to accept false signs of God's will. The individuals might then justify any actions that seem to inspire them, based on a false supposition that their own holiness validates the claim. They may end up going in completely the wrong direction, having convinced themselves that God is with them and encouraging them all the way. This has happened time and again, not only in the Old and New Testament eras, but also through the history of the Christian Church. When misplaced confidence is put on signs or inspirations, either through imprudence or enthusiasm, then individuals and groups can easily go astray.[2]

So there is uncertainty and subjectivity. The process of assessing prophets and prophecy, which helped God's people to follow the covenant, was in many ways a forerunner of today's methods of discernment. The process has guidelines, to be used with prayer and wisdom by people whose lives are committed to following God. The process by itself cannot be seen as a certain method. All can easily be distorted by lack of personal integrity or honesty. Perhaps, too, it is a warning that 'method' can never be enough.

Prophecy and Its Recognition
A key text in Matthew's gospel strengthens the Old Testament

understanding that the source of an inspiration will have an effect on its outcome. 'By your fruits you will know them' (Mt 7:16) is the phrase. The explanation is given that a good tree cannot bear bad fruit nor vice versa (Mt 7:16-20).

How to Test Personal Inspirations

One man who was concerned with the relationship between personal revelation and discernment was John Gerson (1363-1429), who was Chancellor of the University of Paris. He lived in an age when several prominent spiritual writers stressed the mystery of God. Particular problems concerned mystics who claimed to have personal revelations from God.

Gerson assumed that some were genuine, and some were not. The difficulty was in distinguishing one from the other. He tried to write a theology of the spiritual life that would acknowledge the role of personal experience. In his rules for the discernment of spirits he paid special attention to mystics who claimed personal knowledge from God. His advice was:

i. Accept the teachings of scripture and Tradition.[3]

ii. Take into consideration the physical and mental health of the mystic.

iii. Act with scepticism to test any mystical claims.

iv. Discover the motive that makes the mystic want to discuss the revelation.

v. Take into account the life of the mystic (virtue, etc.).

vi. Check whether illusion or diabolical interventions are likely.

Gerson used the same 'coin' imagery as John Cassian, when he summed up his reflections:

> The true coin of a divine cause is distinguished from the false coin of diabolical intervention by its weight, which is humility; by its flexibility, which is prudence; by its solidity, which is patience; by its shape, which is truth, and by its colour, which is the golden hue of charity.[4]

Gerson's suggestions are still of use. If all we start with is an emotional impulse to accept or reject whatever idea might enter our heads claiming to be from God, or whatever idea might come into others' heads, then here is a checklist. Look at the six points to do with revelation, and the one who claims it, then assess humility, prudence, patience, truth and charity. Gerson's scheme concerns, in particular, personal revelation claims, and gives a procedure for investigating them. Gerson does not try to quash personal revelations, nor diminish their importance in spiritual life, merely to reject what may be false, and accept what may be true with more confidence.

Signs and their Recognition

In the New Testament we find warnings of the need to be attentive and to seek to do God's will. Jesus' followers were expected to recognise signs that he gave in order to help them to discern.

Both Matthew's and Luke's gospels, however, give an account of the asking for a sign being seen as evil (the sign of Jonah, Mt 12:39-41, Lk 11:29-32). The evil is in ignoring the sign already present. Similarly in the parable of Dives and Lazarus (Lk 16:20-25) there is a reminder that those who do not accept signs and prophets who have already given their message are unlikely to accept any further ones.

There is a clear instance of this in the Old Testament too, where Ahaz refused to ask God for a sign, because he had already decided on a particular political alliance and didn't want any sign from God that might oblige him to alter his plans (Isa 6-7). So the asking and granting of signs in itself may sometimes be good, sometimes not.

Can something be understood about asking for, or recognising, signs from these passages and those, already mentioned, from the Old Testament? Some ground rules about misuse of signs emerge.

There are five circumstances where one should carefully consider what may happen when looking to 'signs' to help discernment:

> i. When there is clear revelation from scriptures, or from other accepted Christian norms, about what is good and what is bad. If asking for a sign amounts to ignoring these things, then God is being ignored, rather than honoured.

> ii. When, in all honesty, what is stopping someone carrying out a Christian action is not true doubt, but some form of cowardice. It is better not to pretend the problem is lack of knowledge of God's will. A person in this position should try to go beyond a Gideon-type masquerade, and admit that a 'Boost for courage' is a different plea from 'Discernment'. Sometimes courage does fail. When it does, we deceive ourselves less (and don't attempt to deceive God) if we ask for more courage openly, rather than under the false cover of 'discernment'.

> iii. Sometimes, consciously or otherwise, we may use the 'search for a sign' as a way to avoid taking personal responsibility for our actions. We should not, for instance, ask to follow signs if it leads to blaming God for those of our actions that turn out to be less than fruitful, or if we end up ignoring the need for the personal elements of choice, and so refuse to live by the consequences of the free choices that we make.

iv. A wise starting question is, 'What choice is there?' Is there only one action in the circumstances that is good? If there is no choice, there is no need for discernment, and if there is no need for discernment, then there is no need for signs to help a discernment process.

v. Where anyone has strong views or a vested interest in one particular outcome, then there is need for particular caution in asking for signs, so that this doesn't close the mind to some other course of action.

In all the above examples the common focus at the root of any indecision is not the lack of an indicator of truth, but the need for sorting-out of aspects of an individual's life (or values and courage that are in some way lacking). God may use signs to remind us of his revelation, to give courage and conviction, or to help an individual to the maturity of living with the consequences of personal choice. These are great for personal strength and support (thanks be to God!), but they are distinct from those signs for discernment that might clearly point out a truth or a direction to follow.

The attitude we should have to signs is twofold. First, we need the confidence to know that God may use signs to guide us, and that we should be open to such signs. Second, we need the yearning for good, deep self-awareness and awareness of the motives of others, to avoid being led astray by false signs and prophets.

This chapter looks at prophecy (i.e. speaking or giving a message or sign of God). It reflects and comments on what to consider when trying to assess whether a person's message, or a sign, might be authentic.

NOTES

1. For good details on this subject, see Jaques Guillet SJ, 'Discernment of Spirits, The Old Testament', translation of the article 'Discernment des Esprits' in *Dictionnaire de Spiritualité*, trans. Sr Innocenta Richards (Collegeville, Minn: Liturgical Press, 1970).

2. For a good study of how misplaced confidence has, at times, misdirected people, see Ronald Knox, *Enthusiasm* (Oxford University Press, 1950).

3. The word 'Tradition' (with a capital T) indicates those elements that are accepted in the Church as the work of the Holy Spirit, in transmitting authentic truths and revelation concerning God and matters concerned with our salvation.

4. Cited in Jordan Aumann OP, *Christian Spirituality in the Catholic Tradition* (London: Sheed & Ward, 1985), pp. 168-73. For the full text see Jean Gerson, 'On Distinguishing True from False Revelations', in *Early Works*, (New York: Paulist Press, 1998), pp. 334-64.

8

WHAT IS GOD'S WILL?

What God Wants

Clearly God wants people at certain times in their lives to make a particular choice for him. For example, the choice to eat or not to eat the fruit of the tree of good and evil made by Adam and Eve (Gen 3), the call of Noah to the Ark (Gen 6-7), the call of prophets to prophecy (e.g. Isa 6) and so on. Much scriptural evidence can be found to indicate that there are key times or occasions when individuals have a particular choice to make, one option of which will take them down the path that God wants them to travel, and the alternative will take them away from him.

Such choices may, however, be unclear at first. Sometimes the initial direction may even be a test from God to see if an individual trusts him, but will then lead in an alternative direction.

One very difficult passage in the Old Testament is where God seems to have called Abraham to sacrifice Isaac, his son. When Abraham was just about to follow God's will in this, God sent an angel to give different directions:

> But the angel of the Lord called to him from heaven, and said, 'Abraham, Abraham!' And he said, 'Here am I.' He said, 'Do not lay your hand on the lad or do anything to him; for now I know that you fear God, seeing you have not withheld your son, your only son, from me.'
> (Gen 22:11-12)

Here the whole sequence seems to give the better picture (though still not easy to comprehend) than merely looking at God's request that Abraham kill Isaac. Even when we do look at the whole picture we still wonder how God apparently asked a father to murder his son. We see God asking murder, which his own commandments prohibit. Looking only at this part of the story is totally confusing.

When we look to see how 'God's plan' is presented in the scriptures, it is sometimes obvious, yet sometimes far from clear. Looking at longer passages of scripture may give better insight than looking at shorter ones. Even with a broad reflection, some things remain obscure. In our lives, too, there are likely to be aspects that remain obscure.

God's Will

Both phrases, 'God's will' and 'God's plan', are open to several interpretations. How might we understand the phrase 'God's will'? At one end of the spectrum, all that happens in the world is not prevented by God. He is all-powerful so he could prevent anything he wanted. What happens, therefore, happens with the permission of God. That which he allows to happen, however, can include all sorts of evil. When we speak of God's 'permissive will' (i.e. what he allows), we don't necessarily mean what he would *want* to happen.

At the other end of the spectrum, when we speak of that which God would most want to happen, we also call that his 'will'. As God calls us individually and as a community of love, there are some decisions and actions that he wants us to make or do. Those things that build up his kingdom and lead to our repentance of sin, our turning to God, and our salvation, are the things God wants to happen.[1]

God's Plan

The phrase 'God's plan' is also difficult to pin down when examined closely. In part, this term is interchangeable with 'God's will', but it may be used more to refer to particular sets of circumstances or courses of action.

If God has a call or vocation for me, how much of my life does God plan? Is God's plan like an architect's plan for a building, where each brick is necessary, and the size of each roof tile is specified to the nearest millimetre? Perhaps God's plan is more like a strategy for a football team, with God as the coach. Important factors are the players' determination, gifts, teamwork and understanding of the game, and also their knowledge of the opposition. Players in the game have been prepared beforehand and, once involved with the game, have only an occasional shout to and from the coach, as he encourages them from the touchline.

Or we could compare God's plan to the parents' ambition for their child. Wanting the child to grow, to be happy, to have joy, to do what is right, are the norms for a parent-child relationship, whereas a plan that a child must be a brain surgeon would seem quite inappropriate, more limiting of a child's own development, free will and choice.

In practice God's plan cannot be limited to any of these models. We restrict him too much if we use only one of them. He is beyond these classifications. Each, at particular times, might give us, however, some insight into the mystery of his will and plan.

Practical Considerations
Whether the word used is 'plan' or 'will', some of our obvious concerns will be:

Where in life should we try to be aware of God's plan? Are there areas for which God has blueprints, and other areas where he hasn't? What are they? and why? Should I allow him only into the major areas of life (work, family, relationships), or should I have a wider perspective? Perhaps I should consult God about the minor details of life too. Is it right to ask God what brand of cat food is best for Moggs, what variety of geraniums to plant in the garden, and what colour jeans to buy? Does God play a more intimate part in my life if I do?

Evidence from Scripture

In the Old Testament texts there is much focus on the relationship of the people of Israel with God as a covenant (i.e. God's plan for his chosen people as a whole), but detailed information about God's plan for a specific person occurs more rarely. Obvious cases where God seems to have given someone a detailed plan can be found, e.g. the plan for the temple given to Solomon (1 Chr 28). God does occasionally give quite detailed accounts of a sign that he wants a prophet to make (e.g. Hos 1, marrying a prostitute, and Ezek 12, behaving like an exile, both to give a particular sign to the people). Much more common, however, are details of God's plan for the people as a whole (e.g. Isa 14:24, 25:1, 37:26, Jer 51:12).

God's plan, shown through the Old Testament, even when clear regarding direction, does not usually specify every detail. It seems that God doesn't have a preordained plan for each person, which has the precision of specifying each ideal item and action of every moment of life. At the same time, there are significant key times and choices that are important for each person's relationship with God, and there are areas of personal life that may fall under a particular rule of God's law, and so are shaped in this way by his will.

In the New Testament, because it is focused on Jesus, the nature of God's will in Jesus is sometimes very clear. Not only are there specific things to be done, but they are often to be done at specific times. For example, when Jesus calls the apostles, the call is an unambiguous personal 'follow me' (Mt 4:18-22, Mk 1:16-22). This seems clear evidence of a plan.

In the Acts of the Apostles and in the New Testament letters, however, we again see that the followers of Jesus are often not sure of God's plan, and have to seek it through prayer, discussion and the gifts of the Holy Spirit.

Alternative Views

There are two understandings of God's will in Christian writing. The alternative (or complementary) views can be expressed as follows:

i. God has a plan, but ideally it unfolds as a plan with us, rather than a regime for us. It is a plan not only through law, but also through relationship, which may sometimes focus on particular events. Each of us is not so much squeezed into a pre-existent mould, as encouraged to grow and develop into relationship through which personal vocation, mission and way of life unfold.[2]

ii. In addition to wanting his kingdom to be built, and wanting each of us to travel the shortest route from where we are now to deepest love with him, God makes specific requests. These requests are for particular people to carry out his will in a particular way at a particular time. Sometimes this may be presented as a choice that can be reflected on for some time. On other occasions the choice may have to be made quickly, or the option no longer remains to carry out the task.[3]

Evidence from the scriptures and the history of the Church indicates the wisdom of being open to both understandings rather than limiting personal reflection to one or other. God both chooses to share responsibility with us, encouraging us to take initiatives, and, at times, gives us special personal calls to carry out a specific action, or to make a decision for him.

Human Maturity, Love and God

If I see God as 'loving father', i.e. imagine him to be a parent, then perhaps the way I'm responding to his will is as a child. What might this lead to?

If I give a two-year-old boy an expensive present, and see him carefully take the gift out of the box, lay it to one side, and spend hours playing with the box that contained it, what am I to do? To take the box away and insist that he plays with the toy might seem heartless. Better for me to play with him using the box, and lead him on later to find value in the toy.

Neither the awareness of God's plan nor the type of relationship we have with him are fixed. They can develop or regress. We are aware of different aspects at different times. Perhaps what we grasp first is just the 'box that contains the present' rather than the present itself.

The reception of God's gifts and use of them is dependent not only on openness, but also to some measure on love, Christian maturity and understanding. Simply having in mind a model of God's plan is not sufficient without some awareness of my relationship with him, and the way in which that relationship is growing and developing (or declining). My following a 'God of Justice' gives me a more limited understanding than following the 'God of Love'. Part of the search for courage and discernment is married to the search for a deeper and deeper intimacy with God, who is love. The earlier question reappears and has to be answered, 'Is God my beloved?'

God's Intervention in Details

God's apparent intervention in the detail of life, whether it is 'the box' or 'the gift', which we first grasp, is not always easy to determine. On one level, if someone prone to winter illness waits for a bus on a freezing day, says a prayer asking God's help, and a friend appears in a car, offering a lift, the correct response is to thank not only the friend, but also God. The one who was waiting asked their father for something and it appeared. God is thanked, and he and the one who waited are drawn together through it. This is not something that should be belittled or ignored. It is, and should be, part of each Christian's normal life. It is a constant reminder of a personal relationship with God, and an incentive to talk to him, to ask him and to thank him for specific things in prayer.

There is also, however, the other side of the coin: the immaturity that a concern with trivia may sometimes show. At times, we might find ourselves drawn to focus on some very small detail in our personal life and to spotlight it in prayer, as if God did have a particular plan concerning trivia, and that plan was of great importance.

Some years ago I heard a homily about 'smokescreens' that may occur when trying to discern God's will. The preacher described how during the first day of a retreat, a question came into his mind about whether he should wear spectacles or not. His eyes were in the state where he could manage without them, but they gave slightly better vision.

During the next few days he had pondered about wearing spectacles and about poverty, vanity, humility, looking at the question of 'Yes or no to spectacles' in each case. Finally he came to a decision regarding the circumstances in which he would or wouldn't wear spectacles. This *single* decision had taken all of his week's retreat. His resolutions resulting from this 'discernment' lasted no more than a further week, when he returned to normal life.

Looking back, he sensed that the whole question (of spectacles) had been a smokescreen, a distraction encouraged by the devil to prevent him from thinking and praying about anything important during the retreat. Now some years later he wondered just what more important decisions God would have liked him to be praying about.

Small detail is as often a distraction from the greater commitment to Christian life, as a lead to it. The focus on small detail can be, on occasions, simply something used to bewilder or divert attention, to keep our concern away from major aspects of commitment in Christian life. Often when the mind strays to personal trivia in prayer concerning choice, or decision-making, it strays away from God. We should be thinking, praying and discerning (both seeing and making evaluation) about something more important.

Over-concern with trivia can show a lack of maturity, or lack of awareness of the great things that are to be done for God (either in the world, or in one's own heart and life). Spending time praying about 'what hymn to sing next', 'what clothes to wear', 'when to have a haircut', or even imagining conversations with others, which never take place, can so easily take up prayer time and energy that should be spent understanding and responding to God's call in some much more major way.

The key response that God asks of each of us is love. At the end of our lives the effectiveness of both discernment and courage can only be assessed in the context of loving God and others. Dithering in the name of furthering discernment and courage may result in love diminishing rather than growing. The same is true of inappropriate concern with trivia. It may prevent growth towards God.

This chapter gives an introduction to the terms 'God's Will' and 'God's Plan'. It also returns to the theme of personal intimacy with God, and considers it as an element in understanding these terms.

NOTES

1. Spiritual writers do not use any standard terminology to describe facets of God's will. One clear system of terms can be found in letter 83 of Dom John Chapman, *Spiritual Letters* (London: Sheed & Ward, 1946), pp. 205-39.

2. For an example of this understanding, see Thomas Merton OCSO, *No Man is an Island* (Burns & Oates, 1955), chap. 8, pp. 116-44.

3. For an example of this understanding, see Hans Urs Von Balthasar SJ, *The Christian State of Life* (San Francisco: Ignatius Press, 1983), pp. 391-504.

9

CHARISMS

Gifts Are to be Used . . . The Story of Sophie

My elder sister once had a dog called Sophie, a completely mad Old English sheepdog. Sophie's favourite pastime was begging. Whenever anyone came into the house who might give her something to eat or play with, Sophie was there, looking hopeful. She was appreciative of bones, biscuits and all the usual doggy things, but what she liked best were ice-cubes. This was very convenient for everyone, as they were easy to get from the fridge, didn't make her fat, and seemed to give her great enjoyment as she crunched them.

Sophie would come back, time and again for more. After a while she tired of crunching them, but still wanted to possess them. She would hide and guard them. She would collect half a dozen cubes under a chair, 'saved for later'. Of course 'later' never came. Within a quarter of an hour they had melted, leaving just a damp patch on the carpet. Sophie would be puzzled about where they had gone, and couldn't understand our explanation that ice-cubes 'were just like that'.

Spiritual gifts are similar. They may be prepared for by habitual begging, especially from someone who is known well (God). They often fit the gospel precept 'For to him who has more will be given and he will have abundance; but from him who has not, even what he has will be taken away' (Mt 13:12, Lk 19:26).

As regards discernment gifts that involve a 'choice to be made', that choice itself may be like an ice-cube or like a product with a 'sell-by date'. If choice is not used when given, the progress of time will often oblige only one option and exclude others. Choice (and discernment) dissolves and disappears unless it is used.

Gifts in Scripture

In the books of scripture attributed to St Paul, we find the word 'gift'. In English, this may also be translated as 'charism', as this word derives from the New Testament word in Greek, 'charisma' (χάρισμα). Paul says, in the letter to the Romans, that the gift (charism) of God is eternal life in Christ our Lord (Rom 6:23). This eternal life in Christ, in Paul's understanding, might be seen as the central gift from God, to which all others are related.[1]

Although the word 'charisma' is here translated as 'gift', it can also be translated by other words (e.g. 'blessing' or 'free gift'). The gifts Paul mentions are given to help us to serve God and others, and for the building up of the Church. They are to do with preparation for heaven, and are a way in which God generously shares his power.

St Paul mentions a series of gifts in the first letter to the Corinthians (1 Cor 12. . . miracles, healings, etc.). The analogy between Sophie's cubes and charisms, however, can't be taken too far, for several reasons:

   i. God's gifts are more valuable than ice-cubes.

   ii. God's gifts, though given to one individual, are for the benefit of all.

   iii. God's gifts are associated with God's power, with service of him and of humankind, and with the building of God's kingdom.

The gifts of God need to play a central role in the life of the Christian. It is important to pray for those gifts needed by the Church. It is not good to pray for gifts that would only increase an individual's prestige, or self-esteem, to the detriment of the community.

Paul's Discernment Terminology

St Paul mentions 'discernment' in the first letter to the Corinthians when talking about these charisms (1 Cor 12:10). Some of Paul's gifts (e.g. 'teaching' Rom 12:7) seem to be gifts that develop, like a skill, over time. Others are only for an individual time and place.

Paul's discernment may be both a gift for a particular occasion, and an ability. In the first letter to the Corinthians the gift of discernment might be described as a grace from God, for a particular choice between two or more alternatives, when the selection has to be made. Discernment is portrayed as a spiritual gift to do with choice, but that isn't the whole story.

The English word 'discernment', with respect to St Paul's writings, is most frequently a translation of the Greek word 'diakrisis' (διάκρισις), which combines the prefix 'dia', meaning 'through' or 'by means of', with 'krisis', meaning to judge or arbitrate. The basic meaning of the word diakrisis is to separate one thing from another, though the word diakrisis can be translated in a variety of ways ('making a distinction', 'deciding a cause', etc.). Paul's use of 'diakrisis' suggests the action of making a good selection or judgement between two or more options. 'Diakrisis' is found in the first letter to the Corinthians amid a discussion of tongues, of prophecy, and of other powerful spiritual manifestations in the Corinthian Church. The gist of its meaning is 'a separation' or 'a good choice'.

In some English versions of Paul's letters, other Greek words, too, are translated as 'discern' or 'discernment' (e.g. the related Greek word 'anakrisis' in 1 Cor 2:14-15, which means close examination or scrutiny, and the word 'aisthesis' in Phil 1:9, which means perception.)

Paul deals both with the gifts of the Holy Spirit and with the spiritual fruit. He sees the fruit as those authentic signs of the presence of the Holy Spirit in people's and communities' lives. What seem to be charisms may come from the Holy

Spirit or from elsewhere. Paul concludes that good and evil spirits (good and evil inspirations) are ultimately known by their fruit (Gal 5:19-23 and Eph 5:8-10). Gifts may be alike, whatever their source, whereas the spiritual fruit is a more reliable sign that goodness is present.

A further reflection that Paul offers is that the authentic gifts (of which discernment is one) will lead to the Church being built up, i.e. growing in love, understanding and unity as a body (1 Cor 12:12-13 and 14:3). Both elements, spiritual fruit and the building up of the community, are expected when discernment and other true gifts of God are in use.

Discernment in Paul's Writings and Elsewhere in Scripture
Paul's Greek 'discernment' words are not necessarily the same as Greek 'discernment' words used elsewhere in scripture.

The New Testament expression 'discernment (diakrisis) of spirits' (which can also be translated as 'discernment of inspirations') occurs in Paul's first letter to the Corinthians (1 Cor 12:10) but not in the Old Testament or the gospels. The phrase 'distinguish good from evil' (using the same Greek root word, 'diakrisis') occurs in the letter to the Hebrews (Heb 5:14) and seems to have a similar meaning. We separate or select those spirits that are good from those that are evil. In the phrase in the letter to the Hebrews, 'discernment' is seen as something that is obtained by those whose faculties are trained by practice (Heb 5:13-14).

The suggestion in John's first epistle, where the beloved are exhorted not to believe every spirit but to test them to see whether they are of God (1 Jn 4:1), also indicates that past experience, or having some set of norms or guidelines, plays some part in distinguishing one inspiration from another.

There are a number of sacred books, written before the time of Christ, mostly not in Hebrew but in Greek, that were used by some of the Greek-speaking Jews. (Protestant Bibles call some of these books 'Apocrypha', understood as sacred books, but not inspired to the same degree as the rest of the Bible. Catholic and Eastern Orthodox Churches see some of them as having an inspiration that does make them scripture, and they refer to them as a second canon of scripture, 'Deuterocanonical'.) In these there are more references to discernment (e.g. Wis 9:13 'or who can discern what the Lord wills?' or Sir 1:19 'He rained down knowledge and discerning comprehension'). Here discernment is related to gifts of wisdom.

In the Deuterocanonical books we find the Greek words 'ginosko'(γινώσκω), and 'syniemi'(συνίημι), which are more to do with understanding, being aware of, perceiving, or wisdom, rather than making a selection, or judging. These are translated in some English Bibles by the word 'discernment'. Old Testament Hebrew Bible 'discernment' words also differ, but can imply both 'selecting something' and 'having perception'.

Discernment Meanings in Later Christian Tradition
As in scripture, so in later writings of the Christian Church, sometimes more emphasis has been put on discernment as a charism, sometimes it is seen more as an art that develops with practice. (In translation of medieval works, rather than 'discernment' the word 'discretion' is occasionally used to signify that the author or translator has in mind the art or skill of good judgement.)

The Triple Meaning
To sum up, we can find 'discernment' in three different settings:

i Paul's usual context, which is most often a specific charism for a choice (or selection, or good judgement).

ii. The alternative, which is more common in other scriptures: discernment as an ability that may develop, often associated with a growth in ability to appreciate things that are good or of God, or the acquisition of spiritual wisdom.

iii. The third, less common meaning, can be: 'discern', having the same meaning as 'perceive'.

What is clear is that there are at least three aspects:

'a gift for selection given for a particular choice';

'an ability that develops, or is retained, to do with wisdom';

'a perception';

all of which are present in the scriptures. Each can be referred to by words that may be translated as 'discernment' in a Bible in the English language.

If I use this word when referring to spiritual life, sometimes it is good to pause and think, 'Am I talking about a specific gift for a particular occasion, or about an ability or wisdom that should be developing and growing?' or do I simply mean that I perceive something? Each of these understandings may be helpful in different circumstances and prayers. Often, no single understanding is enough in itself.

Discernment, as Distinct from Revelation

Discernment is a gift of practical wisdom, a gift of a good choice, of seeing what is right. It should be sought and welcomed by all. Care should be taken, however, not to confuse this word with 'revelation'. Scriptural discernment words are distinct and different from the word used for 'revelation' (which is the Greek word 'apokalypsis'). 'Revelation' implies that something has been uncovered, whereas 'discernment' means that a good or wise choice is made, or (less frequently) that something is perceived.

Discernment and the Kingdom of God

A further useful reflection on discernment (or making Christian choices) concerns 'where it leads' and 'how it is associated with the gift of eternal life in Christ'. Choices that are important, and are graced by gifts of God, should be connected through the virtue of hope to the kingdom that is to come. Authentic gifts, which will benefit the community, should be begged from God. When he gives them we must use them, so that he and the Church can be served, and so that God's kingdom may grow.

This chapter introduces meanings of the words 'charism' and 'discernment' in scripture, especially in St Paul's writings. Reflection on and understanding of these is particularly important in the contemporary Church where much vitality has come through the Charismatic Renewal. Deeper, informed reflection on the charisms will help Christians to welcome what is good and genuine in such manifestations of the Holy Spirit, and to differentiate the authentic from what may be false.

NOTES

1. See Ernst Käsemann, 'Ministry and Community in the New Testament', in *Essays on New Testament Themes*, Studies in Biblical Theology 41 (London: SCM Press, 1964), pp. 63-94.

10

THE IGNATIAN METHOD OF DISCERNMENT

Perhaps the most used model for Christian discernment today is that of Ignatius of Loyola (1491-1556). It is a procedure that makes use of mental prayer, and is based on Ignatius' own experience.

The Experience of St Ignatius

When Ignatius was a soldier defending Pamplona against the French in 1521, his right leg was injured and he required a long period of convalescence. During this time he was influenced by two books: Ludolph of Saxony's *Life of Christ* and James of Voragine's *Golden Legend*. He noted that when he reflected on the content of these two books, and on the examples of Christ and holy men and women, he found an inner peace or consolation. This type of peace was absent when he reflected on secular tales of chivalry. He examined his response, and concluded that the state of consolation was linked with decisions that led to God. This later led him to outline a series of 'Spiritual Exercises' where the examination of personal response could be used in discernment. He used mental prayer and the awareness of this inner response or reaction, as two of his tools in making good Christian choices.

His guidelines for practical discernment are found in these Spiritual Exercises, in the form of a series of rules and reflections which are often prayed through as part of a directed retreat. The first quality Ignatius asks for is a disposition to pray. The retreat, using the Exercises, usually consists of thirty days of prayer, of up to four to five hours a day. This means over one hundred hours of making the effort to pray!

Ignatius advises the retreatant to cultivate a holy indifference towards created things, and to have it firmly in mind that the first purpose for which we were created is to serve, reverence and praise God. He counsels that material things are seen as only of use in that they help to bring about those ends (of serving, reverencing and praising God), so the great Ignatian motto is 'Ad Majorem Dei Gloriam' (To the greater glory of God!). Being formed in the image of Christ is a broad aim in which discernment plays a part. So Ignatius includes much meditation, reflecting on the life of Christ as presented in the scriptures. Meditations also consider the end for which we were created, heaven, and its alternative, hell.

As Ignatius' background was military, he uses a lot of battle imagery in his Exercises, and in his imagery of the devil. Battle imagery has the advantage of reminding us that evil is a real force to be reckoned with. (Our own image of the devil may well be influenced by different backgrounds and is not necessarily wrong by being so.)

One thing that Ignatius was aware of, however, and we must be too, is of overwhelming difference between the nature of God, the creator, who is divine, and any power of evil, which is always of a lesser order - that of a being who is not divine, but only created. God has power in his own right; evil only has the power that God allows, and that is rightly often seen as a power to deceive or persuade, but never as a power to 'bring into being'. (God made all things in heaven and earth. His is the only creative power, which is always good, though to some of his creatures he gives free will, so we have the option to reject what is good or accept it.)

Two Sets of Rules for Discernment
Ignatius gives two sets of rules or guidelines for discernment.

The First Set
The first set of rules are for those circumstances where temptation is open and obvious. Ignatius starts by recognising

that Christianity is not an easy option. Two reasons for this are the pleasure that attracts us to evil, and the pain and cost involved in discipleship. Ignatius first suggests that we look at and recognise both of these as influences in our lives. He goes on to show that God sometimes consoles us (gives consolation, when we are aware of him or his gifts) and at other times God allows us desolation (times when it is difficult for us to be aware of God).

Ignatius recognises a tendency that good choices are often made when we are in a state of consolation. This state is recognised by several features. Among these are the love for God, creator and Lord, which fills the soul; being moved to sorrow (or tears) by the recognition of one's sin or by the sufferings of Christ; or the increase in Christian faith, hope, joy and love. A key capacity that Ignatius wants to develop and make flourish in the lives of all is the ability to recognise consolation and its opposite, desolation.

Don't Make or Alter Decisions when in Desolation

Ignatius suggests caution in making decisions when in a state of desolation. He tells us to act directly against desolation when temptation is obvious. Desolation might otherwise be an occasion of changing one's mind, which was previously made up to do something good. In desolation we may also be tempted to give in to evil. His rules say:

> Exercise 319, Rule 6: Though in desolation we must never change our former resolutions, it will be very advantageous to intensify our activity against the desolation. We can insist more upon prayer, upon meditation, and on much examination of ourselves. We can make an effort in a way to do some penance . . .
> Exercise 321, Rule 8: When one is in desolation, he should strive to persevere in patience. This reacts against the

vexations that have overtaken him. Let him consider, too, that consolation will soon return, and in the meantime, he must diligently use the means against desolation which have been given in the sixth rule.[1]

Ignatius counsels not only to act against desolation, but to act against the thoughts that come with desolation. To help us in this resolve, Ignatius gives various explanations about how the devil works, e.g.:

Exercise 326, Rule 13: Our enemy may also be compared in his manner of acting to a false lover. He seeks to remain hidden and does not want to be discovered. If such a lover speaks with evil intention to the daughter of a father, or to the wife of a good husband, and seeks to seduce them, he wants his words and solicitations kept secret. He is greatly displeased if his evil suggestions and depraved intentions are revealed by the daughter to her father, or by the wife to her husband. . .[2] Then he readily sees he will not succeed in what he has begun. In the same way, when the enemy of our human nature tempts a just soul with his wiles and seductions, he earnestly desires that they be received secretly and kept secret. But if one manifests them to a confessor, or to some other spiritual person who understands his deceits and malicious designs, the evil one is very much vexed. For he knows that he cannot succeed in his evil undertaking, once his evident deceits have been revealed.

Openness with self and with a spiritual guide or director are two key factors that dispose a person to openness to God, as is the faith and trust in God's support, even in times of desolation. Ignatius recognises that many of the ways in which we are weakened, and so make decisions or choices that lead to sin, come through tricks that evil spirits, or our own subconscious, try to play with our imagination.

The Second Set

The second set of discernment rules is more subtle. Here Ignatius considers the person who is committed to Christ, to the extent that evil does not seem so attractive. He assumes that demanding tasks are commonly undertaken, despite the difficulties that they bring. Temptation here often takes on a different form. Ignatius recognises that when temptation comes in these circumstances it is more often under the appearance of good. No longer do temptations come in the form, 'Why don't you do this? . . . It is pleasurable, don't worry whether it is good or evil.' The more common temptation is now, 'Here is something that will result in apparent good . . . Why not do it?' (e.g. A temptation that I will be able to bring more good into a community that I can lead or dominate, rather than one in which I am a servant).

We need to become more wise than before to subtle temptations. It is no longer enough to face the attraction of obvious evil. Neither is the temptation to avoid difficult good actions the only pitfall. Ignatius suggests the need to attune the mind more finely to the consolation given, and examine it more closely. Might we be deceived in the consolation that we feel? Might something other than God be behind it? Yes! Ignatius suggests that there can be two types of consolation:

i. Consolation in which there is no danger of deception, where one is drawn wholly into the love of God, without ideas or thoughts in the mind which might be linked with one's own imagination.

ii. Consolation that comes through, or is linked with, ideas or imagination, in which deception is possible.

Ignatius gives three ways of distinguishing these two states. The first consists in asking the question, 'From where has this thought come and to where is it leading?' Ignatius recognises that it is easier for Satan to confuse us (or our own subconscious to confuse us) with the immediate situation, than it is with a trend or process. If we see what is happening now in context, we are much less likely to be deceived.

The second consists in being aware of the action of thoughts or apparent inspirations in the heart . . . are they gentle or disturbing? Linked with this is the question 'Am I moving towards, or drifting away from Christ?' Ignatius considers a person who is growing towards Christ, and suggests that any good spirit leading this person will do so gently, whereas an evil spirit would rather put a disturbing thought in this person's mind. Where the person is drifting away from Christ, the situation is the reverse: a good spirit is more likely to give a disturbing, challenging thought, whereas an evil spirit is more likely to be gentle.

In his third suggestion for distinguishing between true and false consolation, Ignatius considers the case where there has been a genuine good inspiration in a person's mind, which is linked with consolation. He is aware that a common human consequence of laziness is not to be critically aware of the exact time when the consolation is over. It is easy to prolong it in one's imagination, so that personal ideas are included which might then masquerade as authentic (consolation-given) inspiration. Ignatius counsels the development of a keen self-awareness and ruthlessness, so as not to include anything that is of oneself with an inspiration from God.[3]

Within the Exercises as a whole are several small helps to reflection and discernment. One such practice is found in the fifty-third Exercise. It consists simply of meditating on the cross, and asking oneself:

> What have I done for Christ?
> What am I doing for Christ?
> What should I do for Christ?

The Exercises of Ignatius are not at their best when simply read and attempted on an individual basis. They are more effective when used in a retreat (if not a thirty-day retreat, then a five-day or an eight-day retreat) or when combined with personal spiritual direction. Once the sensitivity to God and to his will is trained in this way, the rules remain of great help in daily Christian life. Even if reflected on outside the confines of an Ignatian retreat, there is much spiritual wisdom to be gained from them.

NOTES

1.   Ignatius of Loyola *Spiritual Exercises*, English translation by Louis Puhl SJ (Chicago: Loyola University Press, 1955).
2.   Ibid.
3.   Ibid. *Exercises* 329-46.

11

RECOGNISING SIN

The Crocodile

One helpful image of sin is that of a pet crocodile.[1] When crocodiles are small, children may imagine that they would make ideal pets. A baby crocodile is exciting, though perhaps a bit snappy. It does something for one's street credibility, and makes an interesting focus of attention and distraction. It takes the mind off other, less amusing aspects of life.

One problem with crocodiles is that they don't stay small. They want to be fed, if not each day, then at least now and again. Gradually they make their presence felt more and more, especially when they are not fed as often as they would like. The question of 'who is master?' emerges, as if from nowhere. Almost without noticing it, control has moved. The one in charge changes from owner to pet. As crocodiles grow, they become more powerful, until at last the roles are completely reversed. The crocodile is dominant. The child is master no more and has to feed the crocodile or be eaten by it.

Sin is attractive. That is why we do it. If it weren't attractive, who would ever be persuaded to enter into it? There is often a fascination for sin as for a new skill, or as something to give one the edge over others. Like the crocodile, as we pander to sin it gradually gains power in our lives. We become bound by it. It grows in strength, and it becomes harder to resist. Indeed, to do so openly would show a person to be the fool for having allowed it into their life in the first place. This may be an added embarrassment.

In order to avoid sin, or to overcome it, first it must be identified. We have to go crocodile-spotting. Next there must be a clear understanding and a committed decision that the long-term attractions of eternal life with God are more to be desired than the short-term attractions of sin. We must learn to be drawn by the lure of grace and virtue in making choices, just as we were previously enticed by sinful pleasure. We need the wisdom of a grown-up to recognise where power lies, and to what extent the 'crocodile' of sin will inevitably become master if not rejected when it is still small. Even when sin is 'small' we still need God's grace to resist it, and need to rely on the power of Christ's passion and death for victory over it. When sin grows, it further weakens the person in whom it acts. Christ's grace is needed even more.

Because sin is desirable and often gradually gains power in us, we may have a blind spot about its presence in some aspect of our lives or actions. That is because of the nature of sin and of our fallen humanity. Even when it is less obvious to the sinner, however, sin can sometimes be noticed, simply because it disrupts Christian courage and effective discernment.

Awareness of Sin . . . An Aspect of Personal Conscience
Our recognition of, and acceptance of responsibility for, sin is integral to God's healing and forgiveness. I am led to deeper love of God because of the conversion of life that so often starts simply by me 'owning' my sin. In the gospel, the tax-collecting sinner, who knows his sin, is compared with the Pharisee who seems virtuous, but is blind to sin (Lk 18:13-14). Awareness of sin (and sorrow for it) is more important than any amount of virtue.

The origin of the scriptural word 'sin' comes from a verb meaning 'to miss the mark'. (As if a slight breeze has carried the arrow of my enthusiasm from the target and the prize, to hit something else and do harm.) Often the awareness of sin which is required is like that of an archer who puts a wet finger in the air to sense the wind direction. At other times it is more like recognising the right target, and setting the right trajectory for the arrow. On other occasions conscience is associated with the training and the hours of practice that need to be put in so that there is enough strength in the archer's arm to draw the bow.

Sin and the Human Sciences

Today the human sciences (psychology, anthropology and sociology) have given many people keys to help recognise, understand, heal and resolve problems and hang-ups in personality, to understand the functioning of a society or community, and to recognise human drives and emotions. They are rightly to be valued.

Many personality problems can be helped by coming to an awareness of the nature of human behaviour and to an understanding of what creates tension in relationships, unwanted behaviour patterns and other problems. The blessings of these sciences, however, are not sometimes without their limitations and potential difficulties.

They can mask the awareness of sin, by using models of 'behaviour, stimulus and response' (and guilt) to the exclusion of models of 'grace, virtue and sin'. Sometimes it may be a struggle to differentiate that 'action or omission' which has, at its roots, some incompleteness, frailty or shortcoming that can be worked-through, healed or eliminated in human fashion, from that which is caused by the attraction of evil. The notions of a 'personality imbalance' or a 'neurosis' are models that can confuse or mislead us when we try to recognise personal sin and response to grace.

At the same time, such awareness through human sciences can help to resolve the confusion between an unhealthy feeling of guilt (in which, perhaps, no sin is involved) and actual sin and the type of guilt that should rightly be associated with sin. Conscience can be misled in either direction (seeing sin where there is none or vice versa); or be clarified in its vision by use of these sciences.

The very language that we use may carry within it biased ideas of the good or evil, and the human dynamic, in any individual's action or endeavour. All language is open to emotive overtones, and may carry secondary meanings, but these cause particular problems when language relates to religion and the human sciences.

An event that one person may call 'celebrating a feast', is described by another as 'satisfying a healthy appetite', by someone else as 'doing some comfort eating', and by a fourth person as 'indulging in the sin of gluttony'. It is often difficult to separate the truth of an action, in God's eyes, from the habitual language for that action in the society in which we live, or from the mind of the one who carries out the action. This, in turn, makes the recognition of motive and responsibility more difficult to see clearly.

Saint Catherine of Sienna, a great spiritual writer of the fourteenth century, was careful to associate self-knowledge with knowledge of God and with the habit of prayer. It is a good union to keep in mind and practice. An example of this is found in her 'Dialogue'. (She writes as if God is speaking to her):

> The soul, then, should season her self-knowledge with knowledge of my goodness, and her knowledge of me with self-knowledge. In this way vocal prayer will profit the soul who practises it and will please me.[2]

Catherine, in many of her writings, linked this double knowledge and practice of prayer with the further element of active love of neighbour. She showed great wisdom in looking at all these aspects together (knowledge of God, knowledge of self, prayer, and active love of God and neighbour) and not in isolation. They are component elements in spiritual growth. It is wise to look at the broad picture, made of all its component parts, before focusing on one or other of these in isolation.

Wholeness
We live in a society where an individual's values and human psychological balance are frequently taken as a touchstone of spiritual 'wholeness'. Submission to God and freedom from the bonds of sin are often, sadly, ignored or put in second place. It is a muddled world. A glance at the biographies of so many of those

who have been exalted as 'saints', however, shows clearly that neuroses are no block to sanctity. Even the patron saint of moral theologians, St Alphonsus, towards the end of his life developed scruples that would put most neurotics (and especially those whose neuroses show in scruples) to shame.

But there is another side of the coin, revealed in the light of an examination of my own generosity. If I am giving myself to God, then I want to give my best self, the self that is closest to the 'me' I would like to be . . . not the self that is limited by fears and neuroses.

This means that we should recognise the things we do that are less than ideal. It is wise to use human wisdom, in addition to God's grace, so that more talents can be used for God's work. All other things being equal, it is better to have a balanced view and approach to life, rather than one distorted by hang-ups.

Overcoming Addictions of Sin . . . The Twelve-Step Model

One good modern 'journey', which integrates good human sciences and good spirituality, is the twelve-step programme.

St Paul, in his letter to the Romans, sums up several aspects of habitual sin well:

> I do not understand my own actions. For I do not do what I want, but I do the very thing I hate. Now if I do what I do not want, I agree that the law is good. So then it is no longer I that do it, but sin which dwells within me. For I know that nothing good dwells within me, that is, in my flesh. I can will what is right, but I cannot do it. For I do not do the good I want, but the evil I do not want is what I do. Now if I do what I do not want, it is no longer I that do it, but sin which dwells within me. So I find it to be a law that when I want to do right, evil lies close at hand. For I delight in the law of God, in my inmost self, but I see in my members another law at war

with the law of my mind and making me captive to the law of sin which dwells in my members. (Rom 7: 15-23)

It is as though we are hooked on sin, or to apparent attributes or benefits that the sin brings with it.

An addiction can be described as a habit, over which one may seem powerless, involving a procedure that the addicted mind claims can bring about a solution in one's life, whilst in reality it increases the problem. If addiction is seen in this light, many habitual sins fall into the 'addiction' category.

The twelve-step programme is, for us, not intended to replace but to supplement the traditional Christian spiritual weapons of prayer, sacraments and other spiritual disciplines. This programme was first developed by Alcoholics Anonymous[3] as a response to the addiction of alcoholism, then was used more widely for other obsessions, compulsions and addictions (gambling, over-eating, narcotic use, sexual obsessions, etc.). More recently it has been used as a general model in Christian spiritual life[4] to help overcome sinful practices and habits.

The twelve steps involved are:

1. Admit to being powerless over the problem.

2. Come to believe that a Power greater than ourselves (God) can restore us to wholeness.

3. Make a decision to turn our will and our lives over to the care of God, as we understand him.

4. Make a searching and fearless moral inventory of ourselves (i.e. be searchingly honest about what we've done wrong).

5. Admit to God, to ourselves and to another human being the exact nature of our wrongs.

6. Be entirely ready to have God remove all these defects of character.

7. Humbly ask him to remove our shortcomings.

8. Make a list of all persons whom we have harmed, and become willing to make amends to them all.

9. Make direct amends to such people wherever possible, except when to do so would injure them or others.

10. Continue to take personal inventory, and when we are wrong, promptly admit it.

11. Seek through prayer and meditation to improve conscious contact with God as we understand him, praying only for knowledge of his will for us and the power to carry that out.

12. From the spiritual awakening as the result of these steps, we try to carry this message to another person in need, and to practise these principles in all our affairs.

These steps in many people's lives provide a route to freedom, when other paths seem barren. The steps focus on God in an individual's spiritual life, and on community support, in a way that should be the accepted pattern in Church communities, but often isn't.

Implementing these norms requires a support structure. It is often too unrealistic to find the strength alone when weakened through sin. The twelve steps also rely on there being friends, a group, or community, that want all to be healed and saved; the notion that 'hope in salvation' can be a purely personal or selfish goal must be abandoned, in favour of cooperative support and a vision of all, through God's grace and the support of the body, growing together, in spiritual life, towards healing.

The fact that these steps do prove effective may be a challenge to our churches, our way of life, our families. It may challenge the nature and extent of the support that we give to others and are open to accepting ourselves. No longer dependent on the benefits of sin, each person with a sin-habit surrenders day by day to God, relying on his grace and strength and on the support of the body of the community and of friends, through whose mutual support, strength and freedom grow.

In practice, the way in which these ideals can be worked out in each of our lives may differ. Not all of us will have access to regular groups where spiritual sharing takes place. Instead of a group, maybe an individual spiritual director is the only accompaniment available. Perhaps there is only one friend with whom we occasionally share details of spiritual life. Perhaps for much of the time the presence of habitual addictive sin doesn't strike us as prominent in our lives.

The well-established tradition of regular use of the sacrament of reconciliation, too, fulfils several of the twelve steps. Step five, (admitting to God, to ourselves and to one other person the exact nature of our wrongs) is the most obvious step that is taken through this sacrament. Many of the others are implicit, especially if we have a regular confessor who is a good listener and is supportive (such confessors are a treasure, and it is worth spending time to find them). The sacramental forgiveness of sins is an extra strength for renewal of life and courage.

Even when habitual sin is seen only as a minor problem, however, and support may be limited, the following are good questions on which to reflect and act:

i. How many people (including myself) know me, not simply by my outward show, but in my sin?

ii. Am I trying to get rid of sin myself, without calling on God and without the support of others? If so, will I now surrender to God and be open to help?

iii. Have I done what is reasonable to repair the evil that my sin introduced into the lives of others?

iv. When freed, will I stay free through prayer and helping others?

Often it is only through an integration of different supports (prayer, sacraments, personal admission of sin, community support, making restitution, helping others, etc.) that sin addictions can be lessened. The first step, of admitting that 'I can't do it by myself', is often the crucial one. Often the mysterious journey from sin to conversion is found on the path from habitual addiction to recovery in a person's life.[5]

Joy comes not through our achievements, but through Christ's achievements in us. Hope grows from a recognition that God can take over our failures and transform them, not from a recognition of any personal strength. Christian courage often comes through surrender to God and acceptance of his support, including that which comes through others in the community. Our freedom flourishes when sin is seen, admitted and surrendered to God, and his strength and support helps us.

This chapter looks at the place of sin in human life, to help us to identify it and to make distinctions between sin and guilt, and between sin and psychological imbalance. It considers the compulsive (or addictive) aspects of habitual sin, and suggests some ways to help overcome such habits.

NOTES

1. I am grateful to Fr Anthony Scott-Parkin of Port Elizabeth diocese in South Africa (and his sister and brother-in-law who have a crocodile farm) for this example.

2. Catherine of Sienna, *The Dialogue*, trans. by Suzanne Noffke OP, Classics of Western Spirituality Series (New York: Paulist Press, 1980), chap. 86.

3. For more details see *Alcoholics Anonymous*, Third Edition, published by AA General Service Office, PO Box 1, Stonebrow House, York, 1976.

4. See, for example, Jack McCardle SSCC, *Simple Steps to Spiritual Living* (Dublin: The Columba Press, 1993).

5. See Patrick McCormick CM, *Sin as Addiction* (New York: Paulist Press, 1989), pp. 146-75.

12

BEING OFF-BALANCE

In the 1970s I visited a convent for a weekend's reflection. I talked with a nun who was then seventy-two years of age and had been in the convent since she was twenty-one. Within five minutes I sensed that she wasn't at ease. She soon explained why.

Aged eighteen, she had felt that God might be calling her to be a nun. She had made some initial enquiries, but then had done nothing more about it for three years. When she did enter the convent, the superior welcomed her, but told her that it was a serious sin to have ignored God's call for those three years.

When I talked to her, over fifty years later, the feelings of uncertainty and guilt from this incident seemed to overshadow other reflections on her religious life. I was appalled. How could any community allow someone to live with such guilt?

To me, that delay seemed something trivial and, fifty years on, not worth a mention. The 'sin' of omission, even if it did exist (and I wasn't convinced it did), was surely minor. I could contrast it with serious sins and evil acts that some of the Church's saints had committed, and I knew that they lived on in holiness afterwards without such crippling guilt. To me it seemed obvious that whatever she'd done or missed in her past, great saints had done worse. Had no one explained to her how St Paul had first persecuted Christians and how his witness to the faith was not subsequently focused on, or limited by, past sin, but rather broadened to see the fullness of forgiveness and the anticipation of Christ coming again? There was something obviously not of God in her anxiety, and in whatever (or whoever) caused and maintained it.

Just as I have been shaken to see how some individuals have spent much of their lives overshadowed by guilt that had little or no foundation, so I have been shocked to see how others have a large area of their lives where no sense of responsibility or awareness of God has been allowed to enter. For some this may be in the area of sexuality, for others financial responsibility, for others it may be some abuse of power over people.

No two people are the same. Each of us needs to examine our conscience regularly, and not to assume that we are like anyone else. But two of the major difficulties in awareness of sin, in particular, are common, and do require a specific focus. The two difficulties have been addressed by spiritual writers in useful ways. These difficulties are:

> i. the tendency to be too lax when examining conscience.
> ii. the tendency to be too sensitive (which can lead to scruples).

Balance in Recognition of Sin

Having a conscience that neither sees sins when they are not present, nor ignores them when they are, is always problematic. The tendency is to drift either into over-scrupulosity, or to be inattentive and lax.

The image of Judo is useful here. The principle of the sport of Judo is that the energy which an opponent puts into an unsuccessful encounter is used to bring about his downfall. Those who are engaged in the sport develop a sense that enables them to put energy in, without running the danger of being caught off-balance. If they are caught off-balance, in the most obvious way their own energy can lead to the fall. In the same way, when my conscience gets either too strict or too lax, that deviation from the balance can be used by my opponent (the devil) to bring about his achievements rather than God's. My job is to regain balance.

St Ignatius of Loyola addresses this in his Spiritual Exercises. Ignatius sees the tendency to laxity or scrupulosity as being a human trait, but one that is used and taken advantage of by the devil. Ignatius suggests that the devil's work is to lead us as far away from the ideal balance of conscience, in either direction, as possible. So he says:

> The enemy considers carefully whether one has a lax or a delicate conscience. If one has a delicate conscience, the evil one seeks to make it excessively sensitive, in order to disturb and upset it more easily. . . If one has a lax conscience, the enemy endeavours to make it more so. Thus, if before a soul did not bother about venial sin, the enemy will contrive that it make light of mortal sin. If before it paid some heed to venial sin, his efforts will be that now it cares much less or not at all.[1]

Ignatius goes on to suggest that we should always try to be aware of how the devil is drawing us away from the true balance of conscience. When I recognise that he leads me to become too lax, I should try to be more sensitive to sin. When he tries to make my conscience delicate to the point of scrupulosity, then I should recognise that the disturbance of peace in my conscience over scruples is not good. It prevents the joy and the freedom in Christ that should, in some measure, always be present in my life. I need to direct my conscience in a more moderate course.

Ignatius has a second valuable insight when he realises that often we may receive an inspiration to carry out some good action, but then not act on it:

> If a devout soul wishes to do something that is not contrary to the spirit of the Church or the mind of superiors and that may be for the glory of God our Lord, there may come a thought or temptation from without not to say or do it. Apparent reasons may be adduced for this, such as that it is motivated by vain-glory or some other imperfect intention, etc. In such cases one should raise his mind to his Creator and Lord and if he sees that what he is about to do is in keeping with God's service,

or at least not opposed to it, should act directly against the temptation . . .[2]

This, too, is sound advice. An unbalanced conscience can play strange tricks on us. The prompting not to do something that we had previously felt inspired to do is, for many, frequent. If followed, it stops us from being as fruitful Christians as God would want. It dampens what should be normal Christian zeal and fervour. Ignatius counsels us to have enough courage in such circumstances to carry out the initial good intention.

Balance in Penances
What about penance? What is the right way to do penance or other forms of spiritual discipline? In the history of the Church, self-denial has always been part of the Christian life, but what should it involve? How can I live the penitential life that God seems to require when the scriptures say 'Wash, make yourselves clean' (Isa 1:16). This is a reminder that we should do something active in ridding our lives of sin. Further advice from Isaiah says:

> Is not this the fast that I choose: to loose the bonds of wickedness, to undo the thongs of the yoke, to let the oppressed go free, and to break every yoke? Is it not to share your bread with the hungry, and bring the homeless poor into your house; when you see the naked, to cover him, and not to hide yourself from your own flesh? (Isa 58:6-7)

However, as with other spiritual awareness, the recognition of the call to do penance can become unbalanced.

Too Much Washing . . .
Every now and again people's approach to washing themselves can go astray. There is a curious medical disorder to which

doctors give the name Obsessive Compulsive Disorder (OCD). It may affect as many as one or two people in every hundred. Caused by an imbalance of serotonin chemicals in the brain, sufferers have impulses that trigger either images (obsessions) or actions (compulsions). A common form of the complaint is to repeatedly wash hands, often for a specific number of times. The sufferer finds the practice unpleasant, excessive and unreasonable. It often causes distress, or interferes with the sufferer's family or social life, but it is hard to break out of the habit.

To the rest of us, such habits seem strange. We either assume that washing with a particular soap or detergent will keep our hands clean, or not; but we're fairly sure that repetitive washing has little more effect than one good wash. If we were surgeons, worried about the spread of germs, we would realise that even after washing, our hands might still harbour bacteria that could spread disease. We would know our need to put on sterile gloves before going into an operating theatre. The way of profound cleanliness is to wash, and then to put on that which we know will keep us free from germs.

In some respects, spiritual freedom from sin is similar. We need to beware of obsessions and compulsions. We need to do spiritual washing (penance, repentance, acts of prayer and virtue), but we're also called to realise that being kept free from sin is only possible through Christ, the sinless one, whose death frees us from sin. This is the only way to be 'clean' from sin. We must somehow put on Christ as a hand wears a glove (e. g. Gal 3:27 'For as many of you as were baptised into Christ have put on Christ').

Balance of Penance and Virtue

St Catherine of Sienna gives good advice concerning the relationship between the life of virtue and the life of penance. She puts love at the heart of the Christian life, and puts penance as its support. As she sees it, God's call is to focus on love and virtue before focusing on penance. Penance is best discerned only in humility and love. Focusing on penance 'for its own sake' misses the point of it . . .

> Otherwise, if penance becomes the foundation, it becomes a hindrance to perfection. Being done without the discerning light of the knowledge of oneself and of my (God's) goodness, it would fall short of my truth. It would be undiscerning, not loving what I most love, and not hating what I most hate. For discernment is nothing else but the true knowledge a soul ought to have of herself and of me, and through this knowledge she finds her roots. It is joined to charity like an engrafted shoot.[3]

There is a balance that should be in each Christian's life. Penance is good and to be encouraged, but must not get out of proportion, neither be ignored nor become an obsession. The balance is found both with the knowledge of the good effects that can be wrought by penitential practices, and with a spirit of personal generosity to carry them out, but also with an awareness of a greater overall picture. That bigger picture sees charity, hope, adoration of God and the spirit of service as important components, all of which should be taken into account.

In the history of the Christian Church, particularly in the seventeenth century, views of the need and reasons to do penance sometimes became unbalanced. A clear sign of this unbalance is still seen whenever 'to do penance' is given more prominence in a person's normal Christian life than 'to worship and serve God'.

It may be associated with certain heresies that over-emphasise the effects of sin, and under-emphasise the likeness to God in humankind. It is good to keep the right balance; having awareness of 'sin' co-existing with 'being created in God's image out of love' in our own lives. While it is beneficial to do penance for past sins, it is also easy to be trapped into living in the past of those sins, rather than living in the freedom of God's present forgiveness.

Two good spiritual books, which were written in the seventeenth century and which try to counter any distorted urge to live in a past of sin, are *The Sacrament of the Present Moment* by Jean-Pierre de Caussade[4] and *The Practice of the Presence of God*, by Brother Lawrence.[5] They both respond to an excessive desire to do penance by reflecting on themes such as 'How can I best serve God in what I do today?' and 'How can I be most aware of God and worship him now?' The focus on serving God at the present moment is appropriate when trying to put penance in perspective.

The difficulty of what penance to do is at its greatest when it is a decision I make without reference to others. Where a penance is given by a confessor, advised by a spiritual director, or taken as a norm in a particular way of life, problems occur less often. When I make up my own mind on such a discipline, whether for a season (e.g. for Lent) or for a particular reason or purpose, then more discernment and self-awareness is often required. I need to ask 'What prompts me to do this?' If the answer is 'Self-esteem' or 'Just for the sake of doing penance', then there is something wrong. If it is discerned as part of a life of adoration, hope, charity and service, then penance may be part of a path that leads to grace and blessings.

This chapter looks at Ignatius' model for maintaining a balanced perspective on sin. It looks also at the balance needed when determining personal penances and other forms of spiritual discipline.

NOTES

1.   St Ignatius of Loyola, *Spiritual Exercises*, Rules on Scruples 4 (Exercise 349) English translation by Louis Puhl SJ (Chicago: Loyola University Press, 1955).

2.   Ibid., Exercise 351.

3.   Catherine of Sienna, *The Dialogue*, trans. Suzanne Noffke OP, Classics of Western Spirituality Series (New York: Paulist Press, 1980), chap. 9.

4.   Also known as *Self-Abandonment to Divine Providence*, trans. Kitty Muggeridge (Fount Paperbacks, 1981).

5.   Trans. E. M. Blaiklock (Hodder & Stoughton, 1981).

13

THE ENERGY OF PASSIONS

Where Does Personal Energy Come From?

I once visited a family who had two small energetic girls. I played with them for an hour or so, then I had run out of steam and wanted to rest. I explained this to the three-year-old, who showed no signs of wanting to slow down herself. 'Where do you get your energy from?' I asked her. She replied 'Jesus', and ran off to see if there was anyone with more stamina who would play with her.

Her reply was so simple. Yes, I thought, Jesus does give her the energy of youth . . . but not all energy in life comes from him. Sometimes energy from other sources gives a vigour, not unlike that of a child, to impel us into action. Any drive or passion can be united either with Jesus or with sin. I have a strength to do things which comes from God; but I may also have a passion for sinful activity, which has the apparent same strength.

Sins and Virtues

One of the well-known contrasts between sin and virtue is found in the 'penny catechism' which used to be taught in primary schools. Each of the seven deadly sins was contrasted with a virtue:[1]

Sins	Contrasting Virtues
1. Pride	Humility
2. Covetousness	Liberality (Open-handedness)
3. Lust	Chastity
4. Anger	Meekness
5. Gluttony	Temperance
6. Envy	Brotherly love
7. Sloth (Laziness)	Diligence

The list that we now have as the 'seven deadly sins' (or 'seven capital sins') comes from a selection of vices listed by St Gregory the Great (540-604). He writes:

> The leader of the devil's army is pride, whose progeny are the seven principal vices . . . Certainly the root of all evils is pride, of which scripture says, 'Pride is the origin of all sin' (Eccl 10:15). The first of her progeny are certainly the seven principal vices which came forth from the virulent root, namely vainglory, envy, anger, sloth, avarice, gluttony, lust. And because he grieved at our being held captive by pride's seven vices, our redeemer wages a spiritual war of liberation for us, filled with a spirit of a sevenfold grace.[2]

Gregory took his understanding of vice (which developed into our understanding of serious sin) from the writings of monks from the East concerning images that rouse our passions.

Typically, one early understanding of the monastic life was to go into the desert 'to do battle with demons'. One monk, Evagrius (or Evagrios) Ponticus (345-399), following such a model, gave a focus to this spiritual battle, seeing it as a defending of the self against the evil images or thoughts that the demons used to attack him. He listed these evil or tempting mental images as:

gluttony
lust
avarice
dejection
anger
despondency
vainglory
pride.[3]

He noted that these impulses, sent by demons, rouse the passions in a way that biases our true perception of things, and he gave examples of how we should be aware that this process is happening.

> For example, if the face of a person who has done me harm or insulted me appears in my mind, I recognise the demon of rancour approaching. . . . In the same way with other thoughts, we can infer from the object appearing in our mind which demon is close at hand, suggesting that object to us. I do not say that all thoughts of such things come from the demons; for when the intellect is activated by man it is its nature to bring forth the images of past events. But all thoughts producing anger or desire in a way that is contrary to nature are caused by demons.[4]

Evagrius envisages demons giving us energy, and agitating our passions, to sway them away from the true vision of things. (The same insight is seen in the popular modern writer, C. S. Lewis, in his book *The Screwtape Letters*.[5]) When there is an attraction of sin, which we consent to, then there is more harmful force in our passions.

Evagrius' model of sin can be seen in terms of a gradual process, initiated by evil spirits, to which we might give consent.[6] First an image or thought comes to me that has the potential to lead to evil. I have a choice about whether to entertain that thought in my mind. If I consent to entertain it, then my perception of what is desirable may be swayed from that which is good, to that which is not. My passions can be roused to pursue the attraction of the evil, rather than the good, and acts of sin may follow.

As the process evolves, so the personal energy and courage that should be fired by the desire for what is good is warped or distorted. Personal good energy starts to be sapped before the act of sin. As I either become inattentive to thoughts that impinge on my mind, or grow wearied in grappling with them, so vitality and drive to do good may become diminished.

Evagrius counsels a life of spiritual discipline (simplicity, poverty, penance, etc.). This is to strengthen the self-discipline needed to stop sin getting a hold on us. He also advocates prayer and humility as supporting weapons in the fight.

Awareness of the Source of Personal Energies

One aspect of this understanding can help us to be aware of personal sin. Sin can often be recognised by examining a personal response or reaction that seems to be beyond what the circumstances warrant.

An example is where my passion is roused to condemn another's faults. When this urge is brought on by a sinful passion I am unlikely to be aware that I want to spend eternity with this person in heaven, nor to have compassion for them, nor to want to help them, but only to be fuelled by excessive anger.

Not only might 'extra' energy come from anger, but it may come from any serious sin, sometimes in an obvious way, sometimes disguised as indignation, righteousness, concern for others, or by a myriad of other masks.

Sin flows from images and feelings that arouse our emotions in an unbalanced way. In such circumstances the realisation of our God-given 'purpose' here on earth is often forgotten. We are here to make choices for good and to put them into practice. The free choices we make are between the attraction to God and the attraction to evil. Unbalanced passions make free choices more difficult. God is the one who should be the focus of the energy of our passions,[7] so it is not surprising that if my passions are diverted from virtue to vice, there is either an unbalance or a dullness about my response to grace.

Passions are an amalgam of our imagination and feelings. It is clear that the information which these give is not always reliable and may not provide a true awareness of God. Many spiritual writers have noted that passions are harmed and weakened through the effects of sin in our lives (both actual sin and Original Sin). For example, the anonymous English fourteenth-century author of *The Cloud of Unknowing* writes about neophytes (recent converts to Christianity):

> Before Original Sin, imagination co-operated completely with Reason. Like a handmaid it faithfully reflected each image as it really was and thus Reason was never deceived in its judgements by the distorted likeness of any material or spiritual thing. Now, however, this integrity of our nature is lost, and imagination never ceases day or night to distort the image of material creatures, to create counterfeits of their spiritual essences or to conjure up fantasies of spiritual things in our minds. Without the help of Grace it is liable to great error in perceiving and thus produces many counterfeits of reality.[8]

Such understanding of the passions (of our imagination and feelings) reminds us of the need for caution, and for recognising how easy it is to be led astray. The implications of this are obvious in carrying out a regular examination of conscience. Here the practice of reflecting on any roused passions can be useful, asking how they have been roused. (Is it by images of things that do not lead to God?)

Recognising Paths that lead to Sin, and to God

St Francis de Sales, writing in the early seventeenth century, suggested that the sequence by which we are led to virtue is similar to the sequence that leads to sin. He said:

> To complete a marriage, three steps are necessary. One proposes, the other approves, and together they consent. In the same way, when God wishes to perform some great act

of love in us, by us or with us, he first proposes it to us by inspiration, secondly we approve it, and thirdly we consent to it. There are three steps through which we descend to sin – temptation, delight and consent. Likewise, there are three steps by which we rise to virtue: inspiration which is contrary to temptation, delight taken in the inspiration as opposed to the delight found in temptation, and consent to the inspiration which is contrary to the consent to temptation.[9]

An understanding of temptation can lead us also to a greater understanding of how God wants to work in our lives. A greater awareness of one is linked with a greater perception of the other. This combined awareness is more powerful than seeing one sequence, either towards God or away from him, in isolation. The understanding of how the path to sin binds us can strengthen the resolve to follow the path of God who frees us. Recognising and reflecting on our passions can help in this understanding.

This chapter considers sin in the light of uncontrolled or unbalanced 'passions', which can sap energy from, or misdirect, spiritual life.

NOTES

1. See Catholic Truth Society, *A Catechism of Christian Doctrine* (London: 1889, revised 1985), no. 324.

2. Gregory the Great, 'Moralia in Job', 32:45, cited in *The Companion to the Catechism of the Catholic Church*, (San Francisco: Ignatius Press, 1994), p. 637.

3. Evagrios of Pontus (or Pontikos), 'Texts on Discrimination in Respect of Passions and Thoughts', in *The Philokalia*, Vol 1, trans. G. E. H. Palmer et al., (London: Faber & Faber, 1979), pp. 38-52.

4. Op. cit., p. 39.

5. C. S. Lewis, *The Screwtape Letters* (London: Fontana Books, 1955).

6. For a good insight into Evagrius, see Simon Tugwell OP, *Ways of Imperfection* (Springfield, Illinois: Templegate Publishers, 1985), chap 3.

7. Many ancient writers had an understanding of all 'passions' as impulses that are evil. A more moderate view is to distinguish balanced passions from unbalanced ones, and to see only unbalanced passions as routes to evil, with the right use of passions being centred on God. It is in the latter sense that the word 'passions' is used here.

8. *The Cloud of Unknowing*, chap 65. (There are many editions. The one quoted from here is Image Books, London: Doubleday, 1973).

9. St Francis de Sales *Introduction to the Devout Life*, Part II, Chapter 18. The edition quoted from is C. Dollen, ed., (New York: Alba House, 1992).

14

THE DYNAMICS OF CONSCIENCE

The Need for Conscience

In Dostoevsky's famous novel, *Crime and Punishment*, the central character, Raskolnikov, commits murder and then tries to cope with the effect of the crime. The first page of the novel gives us a clue to his openness to such an evil act. In his daydreaming he muses on 'overcoming cowardice' as the main impulse that might be a type of 'courage' to guide his life . . .

> Everything lies in a man's hands, and if he lets it all slip past his nose it's purely out of cowardice . . . that's an axiom. It's a curious reflection: what are people most afraid of? Of doing something new, saying a new word of their own that hasn't been said before – that's what scares them most.[1]

He overcomes his 'fear of doing something new', and goes on to kill a money-lender and her sister. The reader realises as the book progresses that this particular 'fear' should not have been overcome. Though Raskolnikov didn't recognise it, this was his conscience.

A Model for Conscience

Conscience needs to be recognised and seen in its fullness by each of us. One helpful image of conscience is not as a 'fear', but as a 'guiding light'.

This image of conscience as a spark or light is common in Christian writing. An example of this is seen in the writings of the sixth-century abbot, Dorotheos of Gaza:

> When God created man, he breathed into him something divine, as it were a hot and bright spark added to reason,

which lit up the mind and showed him the difference between right and wrong. This is called the conscience, which is the Law of his nature. . . . But when this law was buried and trodden underfoot by men through the onset of sin, we needed a written law, we needed the holy prophets, we needed the instruction of our master, Jesus Christ, to raise it up. . . . It is in our power either to bury it again or, if we obey it, to allow it to shine and illuminate us.[2]

In the Middle Ages, too, particularly in the thirteenth and fourteenth centuries, Flemish writers used an image of each person having a 'spark in the soul', which is seen as part of the motivation of conscience, for example:

Moreover a person has a natural and fundamental inclination towards God through the spark of the soul and through higher reason, which always desires what is good and hates what is evil.[3]

John Henry Newman (1801-90) saw conscience as an inner voice. He described it as a 'dutiful obedience to what claims to be a divine voice, speaking within us'[4] and as 'the voice of God in the nature and heart of man, as distinct from the voice of Revelation'.[5] To him, conscience must be integral to all that prompts us. It must be a motivating force.

When 'conscience' is used in considering what should be done, it overlaps with the word 'discernment'. In this sense it is concerned with choices in life that are integral to a person's following of Christ.

Formed by the Holy Spirit

We can understand the spark of conscience as the guiding voice of God (the guidance of the Holy Spirit). It is a personal call, which can rebuke or encourage where necessary.

The Holy Spirit doesn't do away with norms and codes of life, but brings a deeper and more personal dimension to them. The Spirit is more vibrant than duty, more energetic than discernment, more personal than moral and ethical codes, more enthusiastic than prudent good judgement. The Spirit is not contrary to any of these, but deeper. The Holy Spirit seeks to call and form each of us in the image of love. The growth to maturity in love has two aspects:

> i. The growth in understanding, and uniting of my mind and heart with God and that which is good (that aspect of love that is characterised by wisdom, openness, peaceful unity with God).

> ii. The growth in the taking of responsibility, having strength to do what is right, to act as one should, to be brave for God (that aspect of love that is characterised by courage, fire, witness, energy for what is good, what is of God).

The Holy Spirit does not offer us a choice of fire or wisdom, but yearns that we should have both.

What Model for Certainty?

How sure can we be that any particular decision is a prompting of a good conscience? Should we say 'I won't do such and such because I'm not absolutely certain that it's right', or, 'I will do so and so because I'm not absolutely sure that it's wrong?' Clearly such an approach is ridiculous. Human experience shows that 'proof positive' in conscience isn't like that. So what approach to certainty should we have in matters of conscience?

Newman reflected on, and wrote about, his ideas of certainty, with respect to things of God. His images include reflections both on: i. assent to general truths of faith; and ii. specifically on conscience. Both his general models of 'assent' and particular models of 'conscience' have relevance to discernment and courage, and so ideas from each are included here.

One analogy of when to do something and when not to, which he proposed, used the image of a clock.[6] A clock is continuously gathering evidence that time is passing, as its spring transfers energy to the mechanism and the hands move round the face. When the right amount of evidence is collected that an hour has passed, the clock will chime the hour.

The making of a choice to do something, or refrain from doing something, should be similar, like the chime on a clock. If it strikes when it should not. . . it is proof that the clock is out of order. And the striking can be either too early or too late. Both suggest that the clock is not working as it should.

The nature of the 'evidence to be gathered for conscience' is different from that which a clock gathers. For one thing, the bits of evidence are not all of the same strength. It seems that there are various springs in action, some weaker and some stronger than others. We receive, believe, or judge that things are from God, with different amounts of certainty or conviction. With the different amounts of conviction should come a differing energy to accept and hold something as true, and to use that evidence to spur us into action.

Elsewhere in his writings, Newman uses the image of a mountaineer as a metaphor of the working of the Christian mind when that person seeks God. He likens the small toe-holds and finger-holds on the mountain to 'probability', 'associations', 'law' (of God), 'instinct', 'memory', and so on. The image given is of an experienced person determined to climb a mountain, using all there is to help. The track is not easy to see, nor is it easy to teach to others, but all skill, associations and determinations are focused on the climb, which succeeds by use of them all.[7]

Newman's images suggest that every type of belief gives us some energy to say 'yes' to God. That means everything . . . from those things we take for granted almost without question, right up to those things that we've wrestled with, prayed about, and learned all we can about, before having a firm personal conviction of their truth. Perhaps those things with which we still wrestle also give some energy or direction. Each of these contributes to that blend of fire and wisdom that makes up the dynamic Christian life. For Newman, certainty grows through the cumulative convergence of probabilities. When we are open to the truth, and more and more evidence points in one direction, so we grow in certainty and conviction. This growth matures to give a sure conscience.

Such ideas on assent or certainty are useful, not only in the general realm of faith, but also in the specific realm of conscience. Conscience must be much more than 'passive'. It must not be just waiting for events to happen, or impulses to entice us. Neither should it be concerned simply with avoiding bad things. It must give a drive and an energy. Conscience should be more pro-active than re-active.

The central role of conscience is not to focus on guilt, nor simply a 'thou shalt not' mechanism. It is both an intrinsic force and something that is strengthened by all good evidence before us. It asks us to be aware, to be human, to want to love God and to be generous, as well as having a moral sense and wisdom. A good conscience gives us the initial discrimination between right and wrong, and also galvanises us into action where there is a good to be done, or an evil to be prevented.

Keeping Conscience in Good Shape

Dorotheos of Gaza, like many spiritual writers, notes that if we ignore conscience in small things, eventually it becomes dulled and difficult to recognise when it prompts us on major issues:

> From this way of saying, 'What does this or that matter?' a man takes evil and bitter nourishment and begins presently to despise greater and more serious things and even to

tread down his own conscience and so, at last destroying it, bit by bit, he falls into danger and becomes completely impervious to the light of conscience.[8]

To avoid this, the constant personal task with respect to conscience is a triple one:

    i. to form it;

    ii. to be sensitive to it;

    iii. to be impelled into action by it.

Conscience needs to be balanced, using inspiration and being formed by evidence. Our daily prayer and spiritual task is to be open so that conscience can work fully in our lives. We must move towards God, always prompted by this leading. The first of the three tasks above (conscience formation) can, however, sometimes lead to tensions.

Tensions in Conscience
The quest for formed conscience may seem to bring us up against a tension that can pull three ways. It is a tension of integrity. Besides the initial spark of conscience, there are formative influences in our lives that are part of the environment in which our conscience functions. Where these forces seem to conflict, there may be a tension. This can often be due to a lack of harmony between the following:

    i. The perceived formation through Revelation of God (scripture, dogmatic Church teaching and so on).

    ii. The perceived formation that comes through personal factors (personal reasoning, personal background, habits, personal emotive issues).

iii. The formation that is mediated through influence in a community (societal pressure, Church pressure, family pressure, some obligation to obedience, or loyalty and the sense of honour or shame that these might bring).

This tension can be either creative or destructive. It is most creative when we are able to hold all its component parts in prayer, and examine each in God's light . . . seeing the overall tension, showing up inconsistencies, which then require prayer, healing or deeper understanding. It may be destructive when we reject the challenge to see that tension, and blindly follow the single influence of one factor, the others being quashed or allowed to ferment beneath the surface. The spark of conscience itself may be severely repressed if individual influences are not identified or are suppressed without examination.

The dynamic power of conscience often reveals itself through the way in which it at first seems to want to pull us in two directions at once, and the energy it gives often comes out of struggle and effort. When we finally have to admit that we've given too much attention to one influence and have to reduce our leanings in that direction, then a strength, fire and vigour more united to God may flourish, giving new energy to our spiritual life.

This chapter considers how conscience can motivate us. It looks at conscience not only as that which helps us to identify right (and wrong) choices, but also as that which gives us the energy to carry out those right choices.

NOTES

1. Fyodor Dostoevsky, *Crime and Punishment,* trans. D. McDuff (Penguin Classics, 1991), pp. 33-4.

2. Dorotheos of Gaza, 'On Conscience', in *Discourses and Sayings,* trans. Eric P. Wheeler (Kalamazoo, Michigan: Cistercian Publications, 1977), p. 104.

3. John Ruusbroec, 'The Spiritual Espousals', in *The Spiritual Espousals and Other Works,* trans. James A. Wiseman OSB (Manwah, New Jersey: Paulist Press, 1985), p. 45.

4. Letter to the Duke of Norfolk cited in Ian Ker, ed., *Newman the Theologian, A Reader* (Collins, 1990), p. 236.

5. Ibid. p. 232.

6. John Henry Newman, *An Essay in Aid of a Grammar of Assent,* ed. Ian Ker, (Oxford: Clarendon Press,1985), chap 7, p. 152.
   The 'clock' image of conscience may predate Newman. See *2010 Popular Quotations,* ed. Thomas W. Hanford, 1895/1997, (Albany, Oregon: Ages Digital Software), p. 409, 'Conscience is a clock . . .'

7. Ian Ker, *An Essay in Aid of the Grammer of Assent,* Introduction to Newman's *Grammer of Assent* (Oxford: Clarendon Press, 1985), p. xxvi.

8. Dorotheos of Gaza, loc. cit., p. 105.

15

FRIENDS AND DECISIONS

I became clearly aware of a harmful strength of loyalty among friends some years ago. At the time I was a school chaplain, and generally enjoyed a good rapport with the pupils. On this occasion, however, there was a coolness which crept in over the usual warmth.

I was talking to a group of teenagers about the Christian understanding of morality in intimate human relationships. I talked about the right use of one's genital expression of love being within marriage. I explained the understanding of virtue associated with good loving relationships, and the potential of sin linked with abuse of sexuality. As I did so I sensed an increasing hostility in the group, triggered by what I was saying. It was only when I stopped 'giving a presentation' and started talking to them that I understood why.

The reason for the antagonism was that they all had friends, or close relatives, who were living as couples without being married. My audience understood that I implied that their friends might be living in a state of sin. This not only made them feel uncomfortable, but it presented them with an awkward challenge. They felt obliged to make a choice of loyalties – either to support friends, or to support values of the Christian Church to which they belonged. This choice caused personal conflict, and that was the reason for the emerging hostility. They felt a tension – that relatives and friends weren't in full union with the Church, and yet they themselves felt a part of both. They valued Church and relatives and friends. Friendship-loyalty had brought about a strain and uncomfortableness as they reflected on Church teaching.

The opposite potential effect of friendship is the great strength and support that friends can give and the way in which friends can be an energy for virtue, a reflection of God's love, and a great channel of the witness to joy, which we should express. The book of Sirach (Ecclesiasticus) reminds us of some strengths of good friendship:

> A faithful friend is a sturdy shelter: He that has found one has found a treasure. There is nothing so precious as a faithful friend, and no scales can measure his excellence. A faithful friend is an elixir of life; and those who fear the Lord will find him. Whoever fears the Lord directs his friendship aright, for as he is, so is his neighbour also. (Sir 6:14-17)

The power of friendship and of loyalty to a friend can be very strong. This may cause internal strength leading to either good or conflict, or even lead someone to reject what is good. This realisation is no more than each parent knows – peer pressure influences decisions. Formation so often comes through friends.

The view of imperfect friendships as an evil to be rooted out, is perhaps more common in writings down the centuries than texts commending friendship. Part of this is understandable. We are all under the influence of Original Sin, which means that, even with our good will, motives may be less pure, good or virtuous than God would wish. Through Original Sin, some of the spontaneous freedom of love has been lost. Every relationship in which a person is involved has the potential to be an occasion of sin.

The deepest likeness in any individual remains, however, the likeness to God (in whose image we are made), so all that is most deeply human is always that which is closest to the divine. This is why relationship with others can both reflect and deepen relationship with God. If a friendship is less than perfect, it is often better to see it as a relationship with a potential for good, but which may need healing or maturing in the light of Christ.

General Friendship and Spiritual Growth

There are many texts that speak of friendship. Some general themes are now addressed:

Much of the Christian understanding of friendship as a force for good or evil, is influenced by earlier non-Christian writers. It is good to look at the wisdom they offer. In Aristotle's book on Ethics[1] (written reflecting Greek society in the early fourth century BC), three types of friendship are described:

> i. Friendship that is sought for the utility of the relationship (of what use is a person to me?).

> ii. Friendship that is sought for pleasure.

> iii. Friendship that is sought to build up that which is good or virtuous.

His discussion of friendship is in the context of the vision of a perfect society. Only the third friendship is at home in the ideal world. The first two types of friendship are seen as less than perfect, and potentially harmful in the community.

John Cooper, in an article on Aristotle's ideas on friendship, gives several reasons why Aristotle says we *should* seek the company of friends:

> i. The friend acts as a 'mirror' . . . so that he or she helps us in self-awareness (including consciousness or conscience).

> ii. The friend protects one from boredom. This is particularly important where we have plans which are virtuous but are tiresome to carry out. Friends can support our personal enthusiasm and so keep us fixed on a virtuous path.

iii. The friend who shares our desire for that which is good or virtuous can help to bring it about. There is a synergy where two or more people share a desire to do good which enables more to be done than simply the collection of individual efforts.

iv. There are limits to any goodness we each might have if we lack friends.[2]

Another strong reason for friendship is simply so that we may be led into that friendship which is the relationship we should seek with God:

Greater love has no man than this, that a man lay down his life for his friends. You are my friends if you do what I command you. No longer do I call you servants, for the servant does not know what his master is doing; but I have called you friends, for all that I have heard from my Father I have made known to you. (Jn 15:13-15)

As we learn to make human friends in a way that is good and virtuous, this also prepares the path well to make better friends with God. As we trust friends, so we learn more about faith.

Discernment of Friendships

We can't talk wisely about friendship without discussing the two essentials of 'self-discipline', and 'prudence'. To conduct friendships wisely, not only must personal conscience be formed, but we must also learn prudence by experience, to be able to 'sense' the difference between different types of friendships . . . to feel the difference between that type of friendship which is contrary to the fullness of love and that which is an environment in which love for God and others can be nurtured and developed. Key signs that a friendship is becoming selfish or sensual may be:

      i. It becomes exclusive (is inward-looking rather than outward-looking).

      ii. It becomes possessive (passions, especially jealousy, become out of balance and too easily roused).

      iii. It becomes obsessive (at the slightest stimulus, one's thoughts turn to the friend).[2]

It is good to be on the lookout for such signs, and to recognise that all is not well in friendships where they develop.

Another good question to ask is, 'Would I share this with a spiritual guide?' How happy would I be to discuss honestly and openly all that is going on in this relationship with someone whom I respect and who helps to guide my spiritual life? (Often those relationships that we're not keen on discussing with a spiritual director are those about which we're not being honest with ourselves.)

When friendships have good in them, but are less than perfect, it is good to recognise that there may be no ideal solution in some situations. Any decision about friendships needs to involve prudence, honesty, generosity and trust in God. God doesn't expect the impossible – to choose an option that doesn't exist. He does expect us to make the best choice we can, even when no option is ideal.

St Francis de Sales

St Francis de Sales wisely makes a clear distinction between different types of friends. He distinguishes those we have through our background, family and circumstances (who may or may not be Christian – he encourages us not to give these up, or neglect them[4]) – from those we make as part of our Christian journey, whom we perhaps see as gifts from God to help us specifically as Christians.

Aelred

Perhaps the greatest writer who influenced ideas of Christian friendship is St Aelred of Rievaulx, a twelfth-century Cistercian monk. Aelred was influenced by Aristotle. Aelred's three types of friendship closely reflect Aristotle's. He describes friendship as being 'carnal', 'worldly' or 'spiritual'. These are like Aristotle's categories of 'pleasure seeking', 'utility', and 'good or virtuous'.

When speaking of spiritual friendship, Aelred starts off by making the necessary improvement on classical writers – putting Christ at the centre. Aelred then goes on to spell out how this type of friendship can be the source of dynamic power for the following of God's will and the drive to virtue.

> . . . since in human affairs nothing more sacred is striven for, nothing more useful is sought after, nothing more difficult is discovered, nothing more sweet experienced, and nothing more profitable possessed. For friendship bears fruit in this life and in the next. It manifests all the virtues by its own charms; it assails vices by its own virtue; it tempers adversity and moderates prosperity. As a result scarcely any happiness whatever can exist among mankind without friendship, and a man is to be compared to a beast if he has no one to rejoice with him in adversity, no one to whom to unburden his mind if any annoyance crosses his path or with whom to share some unusually sublime or illuminating inspiration.[5]

Aelred looks first at Christ; friendships ideally develop within that relationship with Christ. In this Christ-centred relationship we recognise the great blessing of true friends. Aelred is also very influenced by the joy that a friendship can bring, and by elements of the divine and elements of human fulfillment that come through friendship. We should be too.

Friends may help, too, in other ways, concerning decision-making. Often a better alternative to seeing decisions in terms of 'situations, laws and precepts' is to see them in terms of 'relationship . . . my friendship with God and my friendship with those whom any decision might affect'. This is the way of reflection that Christian writers on friendship encourage. Friendships, and the energy they give, should see and reflect the light of Christ.

Marriage as a Model

One area where the tradition speaks well of the good of two people coming together and supporting one another is in marriage. The image in scripture of a partner tempting one to evil (as in Gen 3:6) is rare compared to the partner being portrayed as a joy, in a relationship of love and duty, and a help to virtue (e.g. Gen 2:23-25, Sir 26:1-4; 13-18, Prov 19:14, Prov 31:10, Eph 5:28, Eph 5:31, Eph 5:33).

The image of the husband or wife is used to evoke an understanding of the covenant relationship of God with his people (e.g. Isa 54:5, Hos 2:16, Songs 2:10), as if the people of Israel will come to an understanding of the proper love of God through reflecting on their own love between husband and wife. Many models of spiritual growth have as their pinnacle the relationship between the Christian and God portrayed as the relationship of the lover with the beloved.

Few classical Christian spiritual writers have focused on friendship in marriage. (Thankfully more interest is being taken in contemporary culture.[6]) One early Church Father who did write on marriage, however, was St John Chrysostom (died AD 407). He saw marriage as a tremendous force uniting society; 'The love of a husband and wife is the force that welds society together.'[7] He saw husband and wife as strengthening one another through faith-sharing; 'Pray together at home and go to Church. When you come back home, let each ask the other the meaning of the readings and prayers.'[8] So he commends regular dialogue between husband and wife based on the word of God, seeking meaning in their life. His homilies also indicate growth in wisdom, in maturity, in intimacy as coming through marriage and leading to holiness.

Some contemporary writers use insights from human sciences (e.g. psychology) to suggest that the vocation of marriage involves processes in the relationship that unite the couple, help maturity and reflection and so enable them to learn and live God's will in the married state. An example of this is Jack Dominion's 'ideal' marriage model, involving the triple process of sustaining, healing and growth.[9]

> *Sustaining:* The couple should be available to one another doing joint tasks (even washing-up!), be together particularly at key moments (e.g. illness, death, but also at joyful and creative family occasions).

> *Healing:* Where there is conflict, discover why the spouse acts in a particular way, which may include confronting the partner with their defensive behaviour, but avoiding moralising. Accept parental roles, help one another overcome lack of confidence and low self-esteem. Face difficulties concerning attachments, trust, autonomy, dependence, maturity, anxiety, and depression in self and partner.

> *Growth:* Seek not only personal growth, but also that of the partner in a wide range of areas, for example, emotions, sexual and physical aspects, intelligence and creativity.

Though the above model does not have its origins in theology or scripture, aspects of its insight may be useful to help one understand the contemporary marriage vocation. The above model looks at marriage as a relationship in time through which growth, unity and shared virtue develop. Family members, in addition to partners, contribute to this.

The vocation of marriage is too large a topic to be addressed in this book (and it is beyond my competence to write practically about it), but it is within such a vocation, lived to the full, that many personal and shared Christian choices are understood and made.

Friends and Decisions
Each of us is offered not 'friendships' in the abstract, but the opportunity to develop individual relationships at particular moments of choice in our lives. We not only receive the gift of others as our friends, but are also called to become friends of others. Friends may be a tremendous power for virtue and courage. They can bring joy. They contain elements that bring us to God, and support us in God's service. They may also, however, sometimes be a source of pressure, making it more difficult for us to choose with God. We should rejoice in, but also be prudent in, the friendships that we share. Taking regular time reflecting on personal friendships in the light of the gospel is time well spent. Good friends are a great gift from God, and a great joy to one another.

In this chapter we look at wide aspects of friendships (and personal relationships in general) to try to understand how these might affect decisions and holiness.

NOTES

1. Aristotle, *The Nichomachean Ethics*, books VIII and IX.
2. John M. Cooper, 'Aristotle on Friendship', in *Essays on Aristotle's Ethics*, ed. Amelie Oksenberg Rorty (Berkeley Calif.: University of California Press, 1980), p. 308. This is cited extensively, and some themes are developed in Paul

J. Wadell, *Friendship and the Moral Life* (University of Notre Dame Press, 1989), chap 3.

3.   See Jordan Aumann OP, *Spiritual Theology* (London: Sheed & Ward, 1980), p. 379.

4.   St Francis de Sales *Introduction to the Devout Life,* III, chap 19.

5.   *Spiritual Friendship,* 2:9-10, trans. Mary Eugenia Laker (Kalamazoo, Michigan: Cistercian Publications, 1977).

6.   See, for example the document of Pope John Paul II on marriage, *Familiaris Consortio,* promulgated in 1981.

7.   St John Chrysostom, 'Homily 19', in *On Marriage and Family Life*, trans. Catherine P. Roth and David Anderson, (New York: St Vladimir's Seminary Press, 1986), p. 44.

8.   Op. cit., 'Homily 20.'

9.   Jack Dominion, *Passionate and Compassionate Love: A Vision for Christian Marriage* (London: Darton, Longman & Todd, 1991), pp. 59-88. For further reading, I suggest Paul Conner, *Married in Friendship* (London: Sheed & Ward, 1987).

16

CHRISTIAN COMMUNITY AND CHOICE

Wish Dreams

One way in which a Christian community can be wrecked is for an individual to try to impose his or her personal vision on the community as a whole, without any communal discernment. Dietrich Bonhoeffer, the Lutheran theologian, recognised this in the community in which he lived almost fifty years ago. He gives a caution against wish dreams which spring only from an individual's mind or imagination . . .

> Every human wish dream that is injected into the Christian community is a hindrance to genuine community and must be banished if genuine community is to survive. He who loves his dream of a community more than the Christian community itself becomes a destroyer of the latter, even though his intentions may be ever so honest and earnest and sacrificial. . . . God hates visionary dreaming; it makes the dreamer proud and pretentious. The man who fashions a visionary ideal of community demands that it be realized by God, by others and by himself. He enters the community of Christians with his demands, sets up his own law, and judges the brethren and God himself accordingly. He stands adamant, a living reproach to all others in the circle of brethren. He acts as if he is the creator of the Christian community, as if his dream binds all men together. When things do not go his way, he calls the effort a failure. When his ideal picture is destroyed he sees the community going to smash. So he becomes, first an accuser of his brethren, then an accuser of God, and finally the despairing accuser of himself.[1]

The starting-point for community discernment must not be an unsupported individual's dream. It should ideally come from shared prayer and understanding, the gifts that are present, and the worship, thanksgiving and petition of the community as a whole. The caution is against any individual with a 'bee in the bonnet' about the community, which comes only from his or her imagination.

The Struggles of Community

The community is not just a 'life situation', that set of circumstances governing how people live, but is also a Christian formation environment. It has both supports and tensions that mould an individual's self-vision and vision of God. A community can form me to see myself as I am, and to distinguish self-centred motivation from that which is God-directed.

Jean Vanier, the community leader of L'Arche (communities where able-bodied people live with those who have learning difficulties), offers good insights into ways in which a community might form me:

> Some people find it impossible to be alone; for them it is a foretaste of death. So community can appear to be a marvellously welcoming and sharing place.

> But in another way, community is a terrible place. It is the place where our limitations and our egoism are revealed to us. When we begin to live full-time with others, we discover our poverty and our weaknesses, our inability to get on with people, our mental and emotional blocks, our affective or sexual disturbances, our seemingly insatiable desires, our frustrations and jealousies, our hatred and our wish to destroy. . . . So community life brings a painful revelation of our limitations, weaknesses and darkness; the unexpected discovery of the monsters within us is hard to accept. The immediate reaction is to try to destroy the

monsters, or to hide them away again, pretending that they don't exist, or to flee from community life and relationships with others, or to find that the monsters are theirs, not ours. But if we accept that the monsters are there, we can let them out and learn to tame them. That is growth towards liberation.

If we are accepted with our limitations as well as our abilities, community gradually becomes a place of liberation. Discovering that we are accepted and loved by others, we are better able to accept and love ourselves. So community is the place where we can be ourselves without fear or constraint. Community life deepens through mutual trust among all its members.[2]

A community should ideally open up each person's prayer life and self-awareness, and so make each member a better-formed channel of discernment. It can also, however, bring us face to face with realities that are difficult, which we might rather shy away from. So sometimes community can be a great help in personal Christian formation. But when the interpersonal factors are taken into account, understanding God's will sometimes proves more difficult in a community than for an isolated individual. Choices of the whole community may seem even more perplexing. Are there any guidelines to help?

What about Community Discernment?
Since the time of the apostles, each Christian community has had both the charism of discernment and individuals' strong wills, sins and own ideas. We need look no further than the accounts of the early Church in Paul's letter to the Corinthians or the Acts of the Apostles to recognise that these elements have always been present together.

Ladislas Orsy[3] used the account of sorting out disputes in the fifteenth chapter of the Acts of the Apostles (sometimes called the

'Council of Jerusalem') as one suggested model for community discernment.[4] It is a good and simple model.

In this section of Acts there is evidence of quite a serious difference of opinion. Some Church members wanted all new Christians to be bound by all the Laws of Moses, including circumcision laws. Others were concerned not to impose on new Christians more than was necessary. There didn't seem to be a precedent for how to handle this problem.

Here are the main points and procedures adopted by the disciples in the Acts of the Apostles (Acts 15:1-35):

- There were difficult questions with no easy resolution.

- Prayer was the foundation of the discernment process.

- The community made themselves 'indifferent', i.e. they put whatever personal preferences they had to one side, seeking God's will first.

- All arguments were presented.

- There was the witness of the Holy Spirit, who cleansed hearts and worked signs.

- There was silence so that the different speeches could be listened to.

- James spoke, giving a suggestion based both on the words of the prophets and the signs of the times (containing shrewd wisdom, with concessions and new ways, but also traditional precepts).

- This paved the way for a consensus . . . 'It has seemed good to the Holy Spirit and to us.'

Orsy suggests that communal discernment is a good instrument of progress at times of major change, provided that from beginning to end the members of the discerning group are aware of their limitations. There are several implications which Orsy draws out:

> i. The further a person is from contemplative insight, the more fallible his/her discernment.

> ii. We shouldn't expect the Holy Spirit to leap in where human intelligence, working with grace, is enough to come to a good conclusion.

> iii. Communal discernment should be a process through which the community attempts to appropriate the best insight existing somewhere in the members, and make it into the community's own judgement. This is a correct description of what ought to happen; although many times it may not happen![5]

He sums up:

> Ordinarily (not in its perfect form), communal discernment is a dynamic process in which the light and strength of God and the blurred vision of man all play their role. In it a sinful community forms a judgement or makes a decision in God's luminous presence. The final result usually manifests something of all these ingredients.[6]

Key words for Orsy, which describe the process of community discernment, include: dynamic, purifying, quiet, strong; and the ideal means include 'building' and 'liberation'. He suggests that the process should highlight the gift of charity as well as that of sound judgement:

> The bond of a community was never in identical judgements but in charity that covers a multitude of limitations and shortcomings. To find perfection in charity means to accept the wisdom of a legitimate majority, or at times to accept their lack of wisdom. We have to find peace not so much in perfection as in accepting an imperfect world.[7]

Sets of difficult circumstances, with no clear resolution, are common in any community. The bond of any community should be the bond of a spiritual family. Families are environments where wish dreams should be replaced by communal seeking of God's will, where formation of each person takes place through the family unit, where prayer, leadership and honest discussion each take their own role. The test of a family's unity and love, however, comes when divergent views predominate, and harmony is difficult to maintain. It is then that the importance of 'being a family' is put to the test. The same is true of any spiritual community.

One paradox of community is that the stability that the community gives to the initial charisms and vision may often be accompanied by decreasing flexibility and spontaneity as the community grows. Each person in a community is on their own process of conversion and growth, often at differing speeds and stages. Any process of discernment cannot ignore this, nor ride roughshod over individuals within the community. What starts as prayer for discernment (asking God to show a particular direction, or to help with a particular evaluation) may result in an awareness of the need for tolerance, to pray for one another, for generosity, forgiveness and for charity. And yet, as these grow, so too may the broader awareness by the community of God's will for them.

One aspect of 'relationships' is of individuals interacting with each other. The broader picture involves individuals as part of a community, the body of Christ. This chapter uses examples from committed Christian communities to examine the making of decisions in community. Most of us do not live in these 'full' Christian communities, but their experience may often be useful for the more limited Christian communities of local church, groups and families, of which more people are a part.

NOTES

1. Dietrich Bonhoeffer, *Life Together,* 2nd ed., (London: SCM Press, 1972), pp. 15-16.
2. Jean Vanier, *Community and Growth* (London: Darton Longman & Todd, 1979), pp. 5-6.
3. Ladislas M. Orsy SJ, *Probing the Spirit: A Theological Evaluation of Communal Discernment* (New Jersey: Dimension Books, Danville, 1976).
4. Ibid., pp. 15-18.
5. Ibid., p. 28.
6. Ibid., p. 30.
7. Ibid., p. 64.

17

TRUTH AND REVELATION

Perception and Reality

Some years ago I took a course on counselling. The lecturer[1] used an image from mathematics to explain the difference between a psychosis and a neurosis:

> Mentally healthy people know that two plus two equals four, and that is that. For a person who is psychotic, however, although the rest of the world appears to him as it is in reality, he might be convinced that 'two plus two equals five', and can't be persuaded otherwise.
>
> The neurotic has a different problem. He does know that two plus two equals four. There is nothing wrong with his grasp of reality or logic. It's just that, deep down, he's very unhappy about the fact!

I learned how to give names to the strange tricks that the mind can play with people's grasp of reality. Not all that *is* true will necessarily *appear* true to each individual, and even if it does, there may be an emotional reaction against it.

It was a useful lesson, both to help me think of material realities and people's perception of them, and to think about people's perception of truths of the Faith. Not only are the truths of Faith mysteries, shared by God's Spirit in different measure with individuals at different times, but they are also open to subjective perceptions that may be distorted.

Revelation and 'the Spirit Leading the Church'

Confidence in Christian life increases when we have a greater certitude of the will of God than when we see it as 'whatever impulse comes into my mind'. Despite prayer and spiritual discipline, despite using the scriptures and sharing with others, the certainty that derives solely from personal experience (or small-group experience) is not as watertight as one would like. The possibility of the reality of God and his mysteries being different to my perception of them still exists. I want more certainty. I want some further strength or grace in knowing God's will, or in knowing what can bring goodness.

What is more, this is quite a reasonable thing to want. Jesus promised the Spirit of truth to his followers (Jn 16:12-15), and it is right to expect that this presence of truth is dependent not only on my perception, but on something more substantial. This 'promise of the Spirit' leads to an expectation that God gives a revelation of truth, at least in important areas concerning salvation, and that this is deeper than a personal perception of things.

How Should I Look for Truth?

In his Exercises, Ignatius of Loyola writes, in the first place, about discernment. Revelation is not his initial concern, and yet, on reading (or doing) his Spiritual Exercises, it is clear that the recognition and acceptance of certain truths and understandings, which come through the Church, underpin his method for discernment. As part of the exercises, Ignatius counsels that one's mind should be drawn into line with the teaching and practices of the Church.[2]

When he looks at the way God shares himself with his Church, Ignatius comes up with some guidelines for personal attitude with respect to God's Church. These should reflect, in personal life, the Revelation and guidance that God gives to his Church. He proposes eighteen fairly detailed rules for thinking with the Church.[3] They include respect for the hierarchical Church, the sacraments, hymns, psalms, prayer, religious commitment, veneration of saints, Church law, use of church buildings, instructions given by religious superiors, good theology, and other Church-loving attitudes. To me, a key rule is his thirteenth:

13. If we wish to proceed securely in all things, we must hold fast to the following principle: What seems to me white, I will believe black if the hierarchical Church so defines. For I must be convinced that in Christ our Lord, the bridegroom, and in his spouse, the Church, only one spirit holds sway, which governs and rules for the salvation of souls. For it is by the same Spirit and Lord who gave the ten commandments that our holy Mother Church is ruled and governed.

It is clear in all the rules that a prudent love for the Church is at the heart of Ignatius' life. It is with Rule 13 that we realise quite the degree of submission he is prepared to make to the Church, and he calls others to do the same.

Clarification is needed to understand the nature of the obedience that Ignatius gives. Obedience to the Church is not limited to 'today's Church'. The obedience is not primarily to a particular personality (though Ignatius and his followers were specifically committed to the directives of the Pope), but to the truth, which he sees as revealed by God through the body of the Church.

A second clarification is needed where Ignatius talks of 'what the Church defines'. In the Church, one obvious difference in certainty, with which something is recognised as true, can be found in the way in which it is taught or proclaimed. Those elements of faith that are accepted as certain are sometimes called 'dogma', rather than the more general term 'doctrine' (which can refer to any teaching). Ignatius knows (as should we) that only a proportion of Church general teachings are 'what the Church defines'. We should recognise this, too, and be less concerned with theological teaching and speculation that is not dogmatic than with that which is.

Just as I recognise that truth is one, regardless of whether it comes through a study of science or history (and any apparent contradiction shows a lack of truth in one or other), so it is with the Church. The leaders of the Church today are seen in the context of the leaders through the ages, and what was revealed as dogma through the leaders of the early Christian Church cannot be contradicted by today's leaders.

The blessings of this are obvious when we consider the effect of mental illness or imbalance in myself or someone else. If I observe someone who has a mental illness that causes delusions (a psychosis), I might describe them as 'a person whose mind is disturbed'. To the person themselves, however, this rarely appears the case. Their subjective viewpoint is more usually, 'The world is disturbed', or even, 'I am the only person who sees the world as it really is. All other people's views are mistaken'.

For an extreme test, the scope of Rule 13 suggests that ultimately Ignatius is more willing to admit that he may be mentally disturbed, or that the society in which he lives is wrong, than he is to disown God's presence in, and self-revelation to, the Church through the ages. The implicit challenge for me when I read this rule is, 'Am I prepared to do the same?' The assurance that this gives is in knowing that my surety in faith and understanding of God is based on something greater than the whims of my mental health, or that of others. Ignatius realises that neither he, nor most of his readers, have that combination of wide knowledge (nor the gift of infallible discernment) that would make their own perception sure. We need the Church.

We need it, *not* so that we can worry ourselves by being anxious about whether we understand complex teachings and ideas, not so that we make ourselves feel insecure by never quite knowing or understanding enough, but to build up the assurance that God is with us, guiding us, and is revealing himself to us through his body, the Church. We need the Church as a support, a strength and a rock.

In addition, Ignatius shows the wider aspect of growing to know God, by including normal activities within the community of the Church as channels of truth. The sacraments, particularly the Eucharist, are a means whereby

God's Revelation is shared with all. God is revealed, too, in the practice of normal generous Christian life and worship.

Revealed Truths in Church Teaching

The Church is one main channel through which God teaches. This has been true from the earliest times, when the Church separated Christian practice from Jewish practice, when she recognised the New Testament books as inspired scripture, when she formulated the first proclamations of Christian faith (creeds), and so on.

The most obvious examples of truths that are accepted as dogma are those found in creeds (e.g. the Apostles Creed and the Nicene Creed). These creeds give a good foundation on which to reflect, to deepen faith, and so understand more of God and our relationship with him.

The creeds, and the inherent truths of the Faith that they contain, give us one very useful check that enables us to eliminate some false ideas from what seems to be an inspiration. For example, suppose I were to have an inspiration that something had been created, out of nothing, not by God, but by the devil. (Thoughts such as this are found not only with some types of mental illness, but also in the early Church heresies of 'dualism'.) The dogma of the creed that tells us of a belief in one God, creator of 'all that is seen and unseen', clearly shows that an inspiration indicating that something might be created by the devil must be false and must be rejected.[4] Revelation frees us from error and from paths that might lead us away from God.

The better we know the dogmas of the Faith, the easier it will be to spot false inspirations that could lead us astray. Revelation in the Church, however, is not limited to 'dogma' but is much wider. The Church can be seen as the sign of Christ's presence in the world. As such, all that is authentic in the Church reveals what is authentically of God. And this includes not only today's Church, but the Church through the ages.

Truth validated through evidence from scripture and history and Church doctrine and awareness, through Mystery and through lived faith and personal experience, has a security about it that is beyond the simple 'idea in my head'.

Where and How to Look for Truth

A sixteenth-century theologian, Melchior Cano (1509-60), took one aspect of the search for truth a little deeper. He posed the question 'Where do we seek the truth?' He began with the notion that every institution (and especially the Church) should have some idea of where to turn to find or provide a background that is true, on which to base itself. He assumed that any group of people with integrity will always be searching for truth, and that regardless of the discipline, or the way in which the Spirit reveals truth, truths do not oppose one another. In his work *De locis theologicis,* Cano outlined the sources of theological truth as follows:

1. scripture
2. the Tradition of Christ and the Apostles
3. the Catholic Church
4. the General Ecumenical Councils of the Church
5. the Church of Rome
6. the Saints of Old
7. the Scholastic theologians
8. natural reason
9. philosophers
10. human history.[5]

His list goes beyond creeds and dogmas. While this is a useful list to keep in the back of one's mind, it is not the most immediately useful checklist for a person seeking a ready answer about whether something is likely to be true, or of God. The list is too broad. It requires much background knowledge and study.

To be aware of all the statements, with nuances, of even one of the authorities on the list would take most of us a lifetime. The list is a frame of reference more for academic theologians than for others.

Most people have the potential to check a 'truth' against their own knowledge of scripture and the faith and, where necessary, to seek advice of someone with more knowledge in one or other of the above areas.

Some sources of knowledge are widely accepted to be of greater benefit than others. Those authorities at the top of Cano's list more often lead to truths of God than those at the bottom; though, for some natural truths (e.g. the truth that the earth circles the sun), the authorities lower down the scale have, in history, proved more reliable than some authorities further up the list.

Cano's list can be useful because whatever learning we've had, it helps us to realise our own limitations. I can never learn truth through all the 'sites of truth' that he suggests. I always need to talk to people who are more learned in aspects that are outside my own specialities. I always need to reflect within the wider body of the Church, rather than my own limited vision. I need intellectual humility.

If we try to follow God's will we must do so as fully alive human beings, or we may learn less than what God wants. We must be eager, not only to pray, but to think, to learn from the scriptures, to understand how God works in history, to appreciate the insight that scientists, philosophers, historians and so on have into the truths of God and his creation. We need to recognise that committed seekers of truth, in all disciplines, are gifts to enrich the Church, the body of Christ.

Where there is union between the different disciplines, then there is more confidence. Where there is disagreement, then that is the time to look at the evidence in the light of faith. Above all, we shouldn't expect that what seems to be a truth, which has been validated *only* by emotions (by the heart), will necessarily be secure. We remember the prophet Jeremiah:

> The heart is deceitful above all things, and desperately corrupt; who can understand it? (Jer 17:9)

Truths, Revelation, Discernment and Courage

It would be easy to look at the advice given above, recognise its value, but then feel overwhelmed and incapable, and give up! We have a need of encouragement not to do so, but to take Revelation and the search for truth seriously and integrate them fully with discernment.

It may sometimes involve study (or asking scholars), reflection, and working through apparent conflicts, but it is worth it. Essential graces and strengths come from commitment to this continual search. Revelation and discernment are complementary: they guide in the making of effective Christian choices. Like any powerful tools, they need to work in harmony. In this way they will enable the full strength of God's grace to work in our lives.

This chapter considers where and how truth can be found, and the insight and unity with God that come through Revelation (especially through the Church.) It uses models of Melchior Cano and of St Ignatius of Loyola.

NOTES

1. Prof. Fabio Giardini OP, Pontifical University of St Thomas, Rome.
2. Ignatius of Loyola, 'Rules for Thinking with the Church', in *Spiritual Exercises*, English translation by Louis Puhl SJ, (Chicago: Loyola University Press, 1955), Exercises 352-70.
3. Spiritual Exercises, 353-70.
4. See p. 69, comment on Ignatius of Loyola's model of the devil.
5. Melchior Cano OP, *De Locis Theologicis*. (Unfortunately I am not aware of any currently available English translation of this text.)

18

IN CONCLUSION

When I was six years old, my father one day discovered me climbing a tree. I had an adventurous spirit, and often ended up in the casualty department of the local hospital as a result. But on this occasion it was not simply my enthusiasm that concerned him. What worried him was the item I had with me. In my hand was a single sheet of newspaper with a piece of string tied to each corner. When asked, I explained to him that I had seen and learned something (or so I thought) about parachuting. In my hand was a home-made parachute and I was going to jump out of the tree, high up, in order to see if it worked. He was very alarmed. I wasn't allowed to jump.

Sixteen years later I went parachuting for real. It was wonderful. I had eight hours of training before the jump. Four hours prepared me for the five seconds on leaving the plane. Four hours prepared me for the landing. I knew that the training would help me to avoid harm and to land safely. The parachute I used was a tried and tested model. I wouldn't dream of using something I'd designed and made myself. I knew also that I needed the plane to give me sufficient height for the jump. A big tree wouldn't do.

The plane took six of us up to two and a half thousand feet above the parachuting area. The wind direction was checked. The jump master yelled, 'Number one, jump', and the person before me left the plane. Then it was my turn. 'Number two, jump' came the command and I leaped from the plane. Then came the reality – putting my trust in air and the thin nylon material known as parachute silk. I was much more concerned and anxious than I had been when aged six, but also much better prepared.

More than sixteen years have passed since then. The thought of putting my trust in parachutes appeals less. I am too anxious now to put my trust in the air and the thin canopy. Part of my spark of adventure has burned out. I won't again see the world from the heavens, and leap out trusting that I will come to land, my soul enriched by that view from above. In parachuting terms, I have lost courage.

Courage in Christian life is like that parachuting attitude of a twenty-two-year-old. I constantly need the eagerness to have a view of the world from God's point of view – from the heavens. I need the keenness to know that the world really is like that!, and not as it appears with the limited vision from below – I need the willingness to trust my life to God, to step out of the plane and jump, time and time again. My life must include bringing to earth the view that was glimpsed in the heavens, and sharing it with others. I take my direction in life based on the jump, in trust, coupled with the wisdom of experience.

In spiritual terms, two tragedies of life are:

    i. parachuting without good preparation;

    ii. not jumping.

The knowledge and wisdom offered by holy men and women down the ages is given to help each of us to be well prepared, so that the Kingdom of God will be built through our actions and decisions. Their advice helps us to avoid drifting in the wrong direction. Their inspiration fosters discernment and gives us zeal; that we might have courage; that we might pray, reflect, hope, trust, and so commit ourselves to choose and select what seems most good, and to act on it, without fail, each day of our lives.